THE REACH OF ART
A Study in the
Prosody of Pope

by Jacob H. Adler

University of Florida Monographs
HUMANITIES
No. 16, Spring 1964

THE REACH OF ART
A Study in the
Prosody of Pope
by Jacob H. Adler

University of Florida Monographs
HUMANITIES
No. 16, Spring 1964

UNIVERSITY OF FLORIDA PRESS / GAINESVILLE, FLORIDA

ACKNOWLEDGMENTS

O ver the years I have owed thanks for their help in my work on Pope's prosody to many people: to the late George Sherburn and to Walter Jackson Bate, the co-directors of my Harvard University doctoral dissertation in which the present study (under the same title) had its origins; to various colleagues, at the University of Kentucky and elsewhere; to those administering the University of Kentucky Research Fund, from which came money for the typing; and to my wife, without whose multitudinous assistance I should probably never write a line. In this study, that portion of Chapter III dealing with *An Essay on Criticism* and *An Essay on Man* parallels in part my article "Balance in Pope's *Essays*," *English Studies*, XLIII (Dec., 1962), 457-467.

JACOB H. ADLER

I shall continue my enquiries into Milton's art of versification. Since, however minute the employment may appear, of analysing lines into syllables, and whatever ridicule may be incurred by a solemn deliberation upon accents and pauses, it is certain that without this petty knowledge no man can be a poet; and that from the proper disposition of single sounds results that harmony that adds force to reason, and gives grace to sublimity; that shackles attention and governs passions.

—Samuel Johnson, *Rambler* 88.

CONTENTS

INTRODUCTION

It is the purpose of this study to offer an analysis of Alexander Pope's prosodic techniques as they varied from poem to poem throughout his career. In spite of all the work which has been done on Pope as a technician in recent decades, this sort of survey has not yet been undertaken. Pope's often-stated belief that the style of a work should vary according to its subject matter, even in the less noticeable aspects of style, suggests that variation is fairly wide, and that a study of the techniques of individual poems will reveal much about Pope's art which has not yet received comment. A major poetic career as long as Pope's would suggest the same thing, though the variety of change is probably not as wide in his case as in many others, since his precocity was exceptional and his verse form remained, almost always, the same. Nevertheless the variety is great. And if it has not so far been adequately studied, several reasons may be suggested: first, the common belief of well over a century that if every warbler has his tune by heart his range must be narrow, that the range of heroic couplets is narrow anyhow, that the technique of a "prose" poet is not worth that particular kind of attention. Second, the twentieth-century scholars and critics who have studied Pope have not concentrated their attention on this particular area; if they cover his whole career, their attention is not altogether on versification;[1] if they cover one aspect of his versification thoroughly, then they are concerned with the technique generally rather than the variations throughout his career—and in any case they are concerned with only certain aspects.[2] Finally, the

---

1. Thus Rebecca Price Parkin, for example, deals with versification hardly at all (*The Poetic Workmanship of Alexander Pope* [Minneapolis, Univ. of Minnesota Press, 1955]), and while she treats a wide variety of aspects of Pope's "workmanship," she only occasionally gives a poem-by-poem treatment, and then only briefly and selectively. Geoffrey Tillotson treats surprisingly few aspects of versification (*On the Poetry of Pope*, 2d ed. [Oxford, The Clarendon Press, 1950]), and his treatment of those aspects is eclectic, if highly illuminating. Both Miss Parkin and Tillotson are primarily concerned with Pope's technique in general terms. Robert K. Root is also concerned with general technique (*The Poetical Career of Alexander Pope* [Princeton, Princeton Univ. Press, 1938]), and while he does go through Pope's whole career for critico-biographical purposes, he treats versification in only one chapter, and there treats only certain aspects (e.g., caesura), and treats those aspects generally.
2. E.g., W. K. Wimsatt, "One Relation of Rhyme to Reason," *The Verbal*

1

statements of Pope himself about prosody lead to the view, still not entirely obliterated, that his range must have been narrower than it is; and the standard eighteenth-century critical views upon prosody (though they themselves varied much more widely than is usually suspected) have offered support to the mistaken idea that Pope's range is narrow, since he is still considered the standard exemplar of eighteenth-century theories of versification. To be sure, the twentieth-century critics—Sherburn, Root, Tillotson, Miss Sitwell, Miss Parkin, Wimsatt, and others—have convinced us that Pope was capable of a very cunning skill within that narrow range; but the range is wider than the critics have suggested, and in any case no one has traced the variation in technique from major poem to major poem throughout Pope's career.

As a preliminary to such a tracing, the first chapter of this study will be concerned with examining Pope's prosodic technique in general, in order, first, to establish the norm, and, second, to describe in detail aspects of Pope's general prosodic technique, which have not yet been given special attention, or even, in certain cases, noted at all. I have in another place[3] given close attention to the relationship between Pope's general practice in versification, his statements on the subject of versification, and general eighteenth-century critical views, showing that Pope's practice, from the beginning, varied both from his own theories as stated in his letter on prosody and from the majority critical opinion of his day, and that this divergence became greater as his career went on. In this study, therefore, that subject will be given only such attention as is needed to determine actual practice and variety of practice, though I have tried throughout to deal with Pope's technique in terms of his and the eighteenth-century's understanding of prosody. Similarly, if some aspect of Pope's general practice has already been thoroughly and (in my view) adequately explored, there seems no reason to repeat that exploration; such aspects will be summarized briefly or referred to in notes. When I have examined Pope's general techniques, then, either briefly or more fully as the case may require, I shall turn in the later three chapters to the exploration of variation in his practice from major poem to major poem, and an examination of those techniques peculiar to (or mainly prominent in) particular poems throughout his career. But it is

Icon (Lexington, Univ. of Kentucky Press, 1954).
3. "Pope and the Rules of Prosody," *PMLA*, LXXXVI (June, 1961), 218-226.

the better part of wisdom for any critic to add that Pope's technique is so complex and his devices so various that further exploration will continue to be needed. This is only another way of saying that Pope was a major poet.

In considering Pope's versification, I shall treat first techniques of meter (including pause) and of line and couplet; next techniques involving words as words, such as the use of monosyllables and of rhetorical devices; and finally those special techniques of sound, such as alliteration and rime, which are concerned directly with neither words as words nor with meter. To be sure, all three groups have to do with sound. But the techniques involved in producing sound in poetry are sufficiently various in both origin and effect to make a division not only convenient but valid. Rhythm, for instance—which is a matter of sound—is inherent in all speech; rime —also a matter of sound—is externally and eclectically applied.

But all techniques of versification have also to do with sense. The danger, as Dr. Samuel Johnson pointed out,[4] though his examples seem not always the wisest, is that one will ascribe to sound alone an effect dependent upon sense alone; and many others have followed Dr. Johnson in showing that different words producing very similar combinations of sound in very similar arrangements will, since the significance is different, produce entirely different effects, or even none at all. Such warnings are undoubtedly salutary. The problem is where to draw the line. I have tried in this study to avoid the fanciful; but since any serious reader of poetry has his own ideas of the limitations of sound in reinforcing sense, no reader can ever be completely satisfied with the perceptions of another.

Much the same thing can be said of metrical analysis. Inevitably there will be variation from reader to reader in the placement of

---

4. E.g., *Life of Pope, Lives of the English Poets* (New York, Everyman's Library, 1925), II, 219-220. My own view would be close to that of Charles F. Hockett, who finds "the murmuring of innumerable bees" onomatopoetic, and who considers the fact that John Crowe Ransom's "the murdering of innumerable beeves" is *not* onomatopoetic to be "irrelevant," because "onomatopoeia can be judged only in terms of sound *and* meaning" (*A Course in Modern Linguistics* [New York, Macmillan and Co., 1958], pp. 298-299). Note also I. A. Richards' belief that "onomatopoeia . . . is rarely independent of the sense" (*Principles of Literary Criticism* [New York, Harcourt, Brace, and Co., 1925], pp. 128-129). Moreover, Pope's term *representative meter* is far broader in its implications than mere onomatopoeia, especially as the latter term is likely to be limited to the twentieth century.

3

caesuras and in the scansion of certain lines. The analyst can only hope that his own ear is reasonably normal; and that his subjectivity partakes of something like that universality by which so many eighteenth-century aestheticians hoped to reconcile personal taste with general and long-lasting approbation.

1. THE PATTERN IN GENERAL

Pope's principal statement regarding metrics concerned the caesura, where his extremely rigid rule, stated in his letter on
prosody,[1] that the pause always occurs after the fourth, fifth, or
sixth syllables in a pentameter line, is simply at odds with all ob-
servable facts of English versification. It is true that pauses in the
couplet are more commonly central than in blank verse; but in
Pope himself one finds lines with the pause after the eighth
syllable:

Musick resembles Poetry,/in each, (*E. on C.*, 143)[2]

after the seventh:

And all th'Aerial Audience/clap their Wings, (*Spring*, 16)

the third:

Offend her,/and she knows not to forgive;
Oblige her,/and she'll hate you while you live,
(*Moral Essays*, II, 137-138)

and especially often the second:

This Nymph,/to the Destruction of Mankind,
(*Rape of the Lock*, II, 19)
Ye Gods!/and is there no Relief for Love? (*Summer*, 88)

Even the pause after the ninth syllable is not unheard of:

Superiors?/death!/and Equals?/what a curse!
But an Inferior not dependant?/worse, (*Moral Essays*, II, 135-136)

nor after the first:

But thou,/false guardian of a charge too good,
Thou,/mean deserter of thy brother's blood!
(*Unfortunate Lady*, 29-30)

1. Pope's letter on prosody exists in two versions, that to Henry Cromwell,
dated November 25, 1710 (Alexander Pope, *Correspondence*, ed. George Sherburn [Oxford, The Clarendon Press, 1956], I, 105-108; referred to henceforth
as Sherburn), and that to William Walsh, dated October 22, 1706 (Sherburn, I,
22-25). The Walsh version is not known to exist before the authorized edition
of Pope's correspondence in 1735, and is almost surely spurious, an attempt by
Pope to attach his letter to a better-known figure and perhaps to support his
precocity. It differs somewhat from the Cromwell version, and I shall mention
it only when it adds something significant.
2. All quotations from Pope's poetry except the quotation from his Homer

5

Lines with more than one pause, such as *Moral Essays*, II, 135, just quoted, are also frequent, and even lines containing no apparent pause whatever do occur.[3] Pope's practice varies widely from poem to poem. Pauses after the fourth syllable, for example, occur in slightly more than 50 per cent[4] of the lines in *Spring* and at less than half that rate in the second *Moral Essay*. Pauses in his three orthodox positions occur in about 85 per cent of the lines in *Spring* and in only about two-thirds of the lines in several of the late poems. His early work shows a preference for caesuras in the first half of the lines (over 90 per cent in *Summer*), and this decreases more or less steadily to around 70 per cent in the late satires. The sixth-place caesura is used for special purposes, in certain passages.[5]

But beyond mere caesural placement Pope's pauses vary widely in degree and quality, for purposes of variety, devices of rhetoric, and representative meter. Many instances will occur in the analysis of individual poems.

Pope also objected in his letter on prosody to the same pause in more than three successive lines, and while his practice generally avoids this lack of desirable variety, there are exceptions. The famous example near the beginning of Canto II of *The Rape of the Lock* (ll. 7-18), where every pause is after the fourth syllable, may be for the sake of deliberate and obvious over-smoothness, which is one of the techniques Pope uses constantly in *The Rape of the Lock*; and, if so, this demonstrates what Pope's versification demonstrates again and again: that he was willing to break his own rules, or the rules of his age, for the sake of making the technique match the sense. But other instances of more than three successive pauses after the same syllable have no apparent excuse; and while sometimes the repetition is not noticeable, and hence not objectionable

---

are from the Twickenham ed., referred to henceforth as Tw. Quotations from the Homer are from the Cambridge edition of *The Complete Poetical Works of Pope*, ed. Henry W. Boynton (Boston, Houghton Mifflin Co., 1903). See also n. 16, below.

3. Root (p. 40) gives as examples of no pause, *Rape of the Lock*, II, 55 and 64.

4. Such figures in this study are based on prosodic analyses of the whole of the *Pastorals, Windsor-Forest, Messiah, Unfortunate Lady, Eloisa, Moral Essays*, I and II, *Arbuthnot*, the *Epistle to Augustus* (*First Epistle of the Second Book of Horace*), and the *First Satire of the Second Book of Horace*; and of *Rape of the Lock*, Canto II; *E. on C.*, Part I (i.e., ll. 1-200); *E. on M.*, Epistle I; *The Dunciad*, Book I; and Dialogue I of the *Epilogue to the Satires*.

5. See p. 35, below.

(e.g., *Spring*, ll. 84-87),[6] sometimes it is both:

To Phthia's realms/no hostile troops they led;	4
Safe in her vales/my warlike coursers fed;	4
Far hence remov'd,/the hoarse-resounding main,	4
And walls of rocks,/secure my native reign,	4
Whose fruitful soil/luxuriant harvests grace,	4
Rich in her fruits,/and in her martial race.	4
Hither we sail'd/a voluntary throng.	4

(Iliad, I, 201-207)[7]

Even here, however, the variation in caesural emphasis and in the rhythm before the pause—three of the lines have initial trochees—reduces the monotony; and Pope's practice often demonstrates that what seems a reasonable rule even to our freedom-prejudiced generation may be broken successfully.

Regarding meter itself, Pope apparently took a more central stand than in his statement about caesura, objecting in *An Essay on Criticism* to both the critic and the poet who make a fetish of metrical regularity; speaking favorably in the *Epistle to Augustus* of knowing "What's long or short, each accent where to place" (l. 207), without saying that the accent should be invariably alternate; and objecting in the same poem (l. 271) to "splay-foot verse," though the context, and particularly the praise of Dryden's "varying verse" (l. 268), makes clear that the objection is to the extremities of metaphysical license, and not to every violation of strict regularity.

About metrics—rather surprisingly—he was nowhere very specific. In order, therefore, to establish a norm against which to examine his actual practice, one must look at the majority opinion of his day—recognizing that the variety of views about metrical matters was far greater in the early and middle eighteenth century than is usually recognized. The dicta which would have come nearest to general acceptance[8] are probably as follows:

6. Or *Autumn*, 8-13, which illustrates another of Pope's dicta (in the letter to Walsh only), that the pause after the fifth syllable can be continued longer without monotony.

7. Another example is *Eloisa to Abelard*, 45-49.

8. Based on works consulted, including such obvious sources as Dryden's *Essays*, the *Tatler* and *Spectator*, the critical works of Johnson, Hugh Blair's *Lectures on Rhetoric and Belles Lettres*, 7th ed. (London, 1798), and Henry Home, Lord Kames' *Elements of Criticism* (New York, 1852); and, among others, Anselm Bayly, *The Alliance of Music, Poetry, and Oratory* (London, 1789); James Beattie, "An Essay on Poetry and Music, as they affect the mind," in *Essays* (Edinburgh, 1778); Richard Bentley, *Milton's Paradise Lost* (London, 1732);

7

1. Use of the initial trochee is acceptable, as in Pope's

Lóst in a cónvent's sólitáry glóom, (*Eloisa*, 38)[9]

but decidedly not the medial trochee, as in Pope's

The whéels abóve urg'd by the lóad belów, (*Dunciad*, I, 184)

O'er héad and eárs plúnge for the Cómmonwéal,

(*Dunciad*, I, 210)

and emphatically not the final trochee, for which Milton was roundly condemned, and which Pope probably never used.

2. In general the spondee is acceptable, either with the pyrrhic, as in Pope's

To the lást honoúrs of the Bútt and Báys, (*Dunciad*, I, 168)

Edward Bysshe, *The Art of English Poetry* (4th ed., London, 1710); William Coward, *Licentia Poetica Discuss'd* (London, 1709); Thomas Gray, "Observations on English Meter," in *Works*, ed. Edmund Gosse (New York, 1885); Edward Manwaring, *Of Harmony and Numbers in Latin and English Prose and in English Poetry* (London, 1744); W. E. Mead, *The Versification of Pope in its Relations to the Seventeenth Century* (Leipzig, 1889); Lord Monboddo, *Of the Origin and Progress of Language* (Edinburgh, 1774); Henry Pemberton, *Observations on Poetry* (London, 1738); "J.D.," Preface to Joshua Poole's *The English Parnassus* . . . *Together with A short Institution to English Poesie, by way of Preface* (London, 1677); John Rice, *An Introduction to the Art of Reading with Energy and Propriety* (London, 1765); Samuel Say, *Poems on Several Occasions: and Two Critical Essays* (London, 1745); Daniel Webb, *Observations on the Correspondence between Poetry and Music* (London, 1769) and *Remarks on the Beauties of Poetry* (London, 1762); Samuel Wesley, *An Epistle to a Friend concerning Poetry* (London, 1700); and, of course, Paul Fussell, Jr., *Theory of Prosody in Eighteenth-Century England*, Connecticut College Monograph no. 5 (New London, 1954).

9. I am aware, of course, that some twentieth-century prosodists, and particularly linguists, would handle scansion and other prosodic matters somewhat differently. But I am dealing with prosodic technique as the eighteenth century understood it—in other words with traditional prosody. I would in any case agree with John Crowe Ransom in his contribution to the famous series of articles on prosody in the *Kenyon Review* ("The Strange Music of English Verse," XVIII [Summer, 1956], 451-460), that the poets in the anthologies are traditional prosodists. And I would agree with Ronald Sutherland in his comment on the same series of articles ("Structural Linguistics and English Prosody," *College English*, XX [Oct., 1958], 12-17), that the Brooks and Warren analyses in *Understanding Poetry* are "striking evidence that the old system works," that while some modifications are useful they will increase efficiency rather than revise conclusions, and that extremely subtle methods of scansion can apply only to individually recorded readings, not to a "universally meaningful" analysis.

or without, as in Pope's

Ŏf twélve vȧst Frénch Rŏmȧ́ncĕs, nĕatly gílt.

(*Rape of the Lock*, II, 38)

3. Feet which would be trisyllabic if pronounced in full are acceptable only if they are capable of reduction to dissyllables by elision.[10] This elision could be of three types: either the dropping of a vowel before a liquid or nasal (syncope), as in Pope's

Explores the lost, the *wand'ring* Sheep directs; (*Messiah*, 51)

or the joining together of two vowels in one sound (synaeresis), as in Pope's

Asleep and naked as an *Indian* lay, (*Moral Essays*, III, 361)

sometimes in a fashion very difficult to elide:

Kind, *virtuous* drops just gath'ring in my eye; (*Eloisa*, 278)

or the dropping of a final vowel before an initial vowel (apocope), in Pope limited almost entirely to *the* and (less frequently) *to*, as in

Yet never pass th'insuperable line, (*E. on M.*, I, 228)
A work t'outlast Immortal Rome design'd. (*E. on C.*, 131)

4. Light feet—that is, feet where there must be a metrical accent though there would be little or no prose accent—are acceptable, as in Pope's

Thĕ vȧ́riŏus Óff'riṅgs ŏf thĕ Wórld ăppéar.

(*Rape of the Lock*, I, 130)

As in this case, such a foot in Pope is likely to occur near the middle of the line, and is particularly likely to be split by the pause, so that the "broken light third foot" occurs with sufficient frequency in Pope as to approach the status of a mannerism,[11] though it is a probable phenomenon in heroic couplets generally.[12]

10. But lines like the following from Dryden,

Drówn'd ĭn th'ȧbyss̆ of deep idolatry (*Hind and the Panther*, II, 633)

where actual voiced elision is unavoidable because the trisyllable occurs after a trochee, are rare in Pope, if they exist at all, and are rare in good eighteenth-century poetry generally.

11. See Root, p. 41.

12. Pope also objects in his letter on prosody to the Alexandrine, but it is of comparatively little significance in his verse, appearing with noticeable frequency only in the Homer. See Adler, "Pope and the Rules of Prosody," pp. 222-223; also Tillotson, pp. 105-112.

Pope's practice regarding strictly metrical matters varied considerably from poem to poem. The initial trochee, for example, occurs in fewer than one line in ten in *Winter*, in more than one in four in the *First Satire of the Second Book of Horace*, with the later poems using them more frequently, in a very irregular progression. Elision by apocope occurs more frequently in more formal poems. Pope seldom employed medial trochees, but he certainly did not avoid them altogether, and apparently felt free to use them for "representative" purposes; and lines occasionally occur where no more than two feet[13] are iambic, or where the iambic is obscured by the complications of elisions:

And the fleet Shades glide o'er the dusky Green, (*Autumn*, 64)

Glance on the stone where our cold reliques lie, (*Eloisa*, 356)
Some emanation of th'all-beauteous mind. (*Eloisa*. 62)

In the last instance, the necessity of reading the third and fourth feet as either a light foot plus an iamb or as a pyrrhic plus a spondee adds to the difficulty. Such instances are, of course, exceptional. Among the more acceptable variants from pure iambic monotony, Pope felt completely at home; and his use of them was full, frequent, and various.

Two other elements of verse technique loosely related to metrics are, first, the couplet as a unit of thought, and of grammar, as opposed to the open series of lines, tending toward the freedom of blank verse, with rime less functional and more incidental; and, second, the matter of end-stopped as opposed to run-on lines within the couplet itself. The tendency in Pope's day was certainly toward maintaining the integrity of both line and couplet, though the variety of opinion was again wider than is usually remembered. Pope apparently made no mention of the subject; and Lord Kames' later view of it probably comes as close as any to Pope's actual practice: "there ought always to be some pause in the sense at the end of every couplet; the same period as to sense may be extended through several couplets; but each couplet ought to contain a distinct member, distinguished by a pause in the sense as well as in the sound; and the whole ought to be closed with a complete cadence."[14] Lord Kames adds elsewhere that this pause may be no

13. Or even one. See p. 32, below.
14. Kames, p. 316.

10

more than that of a comma.[15] These requirements may be illustrated by hundreds of passages from Pope; for instance, the famous "poor Indian" passage, *An Essay on Man*, I, 99-108. And Lord Kames correctly found that Pope seldom transgressed this not very rigid rule. Instances do occur, however, such as a well-known passage from the *Messiah*:

No more the rising sun shall gild the Morn,
Nor Evening Cynthia fill her silver Horn,
But lost, dissolv'd in thy superior Rays;
One Tyde of Glory, one unclouded Blaze,
O'erflow thy Courts. (99-103)[16]

Here the unusual overflow of couplet "represents" the meaning. Other instances, however, are without such a purpose, for example:

Descends Minerva, in her guardian care,
A heav'nly witness of the wrongs I bear
From Atreus' son? (*Iliad*, I, 269-271)[17]

Within the couplet structure itself, a certain degree of run-on is common in Pope; and run-on beyond the possibility of even the slightest pause is less frequent but not really rare. All degrees occur; from complete end-stopping in such a couplet as

Know, Nature's children all divide her care;
The fur that warms a monarch, warm'd a bear,
(*E. on M.*, III, 43-44)

to the almost equally complete pause, in spite of a mere comma, in a couplet where the second line is dependent on the first:

Back to their caves she bade the winds to fly,
And hush'd the blust'ring Brethren of the Sky,
(*Odyssey*, V, 490-491)

to the slightly lesser pause in a couplet where the first line is dependent on the second:

Tho' cold like you, unmov'd, and silent grown,
I have not yet forgot my self to stone; (*Eloisa*, 23-24)

15. Kames, p. 306.
16. Tw. regularly uses the punctuation of the 1st ed. of each poem. In this case (the semicolon in l. 100), and in many others, some of which will be noted, this punctuation obscures the metrical pattern and may even be impossible grammatically. I have followed the Tw. punctuation and initial capitalization; but I have omitted the Tw. italics, since I shall want to italicize parts of quotations (and occasionally capitalize whole words) for my own purposes.
17. See also p. 36, below.

11

to a couplet where a pause seems possible even though the sense runs on uninterrupted:

Relentless walls! whose darksom round contains
Repentant sighs, and voluntary pains, (*Eloisa*, 17-18)

to such completely run-on lines as

On some, a Priest succinct in amice white
Attends; all flesh is nothing in his sight! (*Dunciad*, IV, 549-550)
On shining Altars of Japan they raise
The silver Lamp; the fiery Spirits blaze,
(*Rape of the Lock*, III, 107-108)

or even

From great Assaracus sprung Capys, he
Begat Anchises, and Anchises me. (*Iliad*, XX, 288-289)

II

To turn from those elements of prosodic technique concerned with metrics to those concerned with words as words, is to turn from a group with fairly definite boundaries to a miscellany with no clearly definable limits whatever. While rhetorical devices, for example, were certainly considered a part of poetry by the Augustans, and indeed as a part having to do with "style," they are not usually considered an element of *versification*. Yet it is not only true that the couplet encourages certain rhetorical methods such as antithesis, but it is also true that the use of certain such methods adds a tone and texture which is as much a part of sound as of sense.

Pope himself mentions techniques regarding words, and it is clear that to him they concern versification. In both his letter on prosody and *An Essay on Criticism* he objected to the use of verbal expletives to fill out the pentameter line. Such practice was frequent in the Restoration, but fell largely out of use in the new century. Verbal expletives are extremely rare in Pope.[18] On the other hand, Pope has been accused by Saintsbury and others of using superfluous adjectives to fill out lines. Such a charge is occasionally justified, especially in his earlier work.[19] Yet the effect

18. But they were not excised from the early poems till the 1717 ed. See Tw., I, 199, and Tillotson, pp. 121-123. See also Tillotson, pp. 91-92, for an example of a purposeful verbal expletive in the *Epistle to Augustus*.
19. See p. 39, below. Pope himself objected to superfluous epithets in *The Art of Sinking in Poetry*, but praised the use of epithets for heightening style in the Postscript to *Odyssey*.

of this failing in Pope's versification as a whole is very small. To be noticeable, and therefore objectionable, epithets must be both frequent and either maladroit or unnecessary. Saintsbury finds the epithets in *The Rape of the Lock* frequent, as they undeniably are; but they are nearly always remarkably apt, and their somewhat obvious effect, their patness, seems both intended and effective. The use of the obvious and overfluent is one of the principal methods in *The Rape of the Lock*, displayed through numerous effects with delightful results.

In his letter on prosody, Pope remarks that "monosyllable lines, unless very artfully managed, are stiff, languishing, and hard," adding in the letter to Walsh that they "may be beautiful to express melancholy, slowness, or labour." And in *An Essay on Criticism* he makes the same objection by exemplifying it:

And ten low Words oft creep in one dull Line. (347)

No one needs to be told that when it came to such effects Pope was a wickedly clever technician; and here he succeeds as usual in weighting the scale in favor of his argument. Eight of the ten words receive almost equal emphasis, and there is practically no grouping: two circumstances not quite ordinary in monosyllabic lines, where distinct groupings usually occur in unequal arrangements, and the words have quite unequal emphasis—more unequal than the varieties of print can show:

And NOW TWO NIGHTS, and NOW TWO DAYS were PAST,
(*Odyssey*, V, 496)
SEAS ROLL to WAFT me, SUNS to LIGHT me RISE.
(*E. on M.*, I, 139)

It is doubtful that anyone would remark the monosyllabic quality of such lines as these in ordinary reading.

By the time of the revised letter on prosody Pope apparently felt that monosyllabic lines could express an andante movement successfully. And so they can. There is an instance in the *Messiah*:

And the same Hand that sow'd, shall reap the Field, (66)

a slow line, and mildly expressive of "labour." An attempt to express even the absence of motion is found in a line from *Eloisa,* the quietly lovely

Still as the sea, ere winds were taught to blow; (253)

13

while the same poem offers several monosyllabic lines with "melancholy" effect.

Yet instances of such effects are not easy to find; and they illustrate rather the patent fact that a line of slow or solemn import *may be* sounded slowly with greater ease if it consists of monosyllables, than that the monosyllables enforce a slow reading. In other words, the sense dominates the sound; and it is more possible, when the sense demands it, to linger over a monosyllable than over an unaccented syllable of a longer word. It is true that spondees are slow, and that most spondees consist of monosyllables; hence the inherent slowness of a line from *Eloisa to Abelard* which is beautifully representative of stillness even though it contains a dissyllable:

Thy life a long, dead calm of fix'd repose. (251)

Also, monosyllables may cause a huddling together of consonants, and the resulting difficulty in pronunciation will enforce slowness, as in the famous "Ajax" line—not entirely monosyllabic—or as in the last of the accurately contrasted halves of this line from *The Dunciad*:

Intoxicates the pert, and lulls the grave. (II, 344)

In the last two examples, still a third element enters into the lingering quality: the long vowels. And all three—spondees, difficult consonants, long vowels—conspire to make the following line from *An Essay on Man* slow:

'Till tir'd he sleeps, and Life's poor play is o'er. (II, 282)

But another line from *An Essay on Man* should quickly dispel any illusion that the slowness of a monosyllabic line is inevitable:

Ask where's the North? at York, 'tis on the Tweed. (II, 222)

Indeed, swift or merely neutral monosyllabic lines are far more plentiful in Pope than slow—and monosyllabic lines are plentiful, ranging from 1 per cent of the lines in some of the early pastorals to 8 per cent in *Eloisa* and *Arbuthnot*. They often provide a welcome simplicity:

To read and weep is all they now can do, (*Eloisa*, 48)
Thus wilt thou leave me, are we thus to part? (*Odyssey*, V, 260)

But the word order and word choice play a significant part in this

14

effect, and lines not entirely composed of monosyllables can be equally simple:

I waste the Matin lamp in sighs for thee, (*Eloisa*, 267)
He has a father too; a man like me. (*Iliad*, XXII, 536)

Monosyllabic lines may also be used for a sense of the solemn and permanent:

Ev'n by that God I swear, who rules the day, (*Iliad*, I, 109)[20]
Fix'd is the term to all the race of earth. (*Iliad*, VI, 628)

And while in this case too one dissyllable may appear:

His are the laws, and him let all obey, (*Iliad*, II, 244)

there is a manifest difference between this sort of line and the more aphoristic, even somewhat glib sort for which Pope has remained best known:

For Fools rush in where Angels fear to tread, (*E. on C.*, 625)
The proper study of Mankind is Man. (*E. on M.*, II, 2)

But perhaps the most interesting, if rare, use of the monosyllabic line as a special type is to display a controlled anger:

Glad of a quarrel, strait I clap the door,
Sir, let me see your works and you no more. (*Arbuthnot*, 67-69)

Here the separateness of each word aids in conveying a kind of slow, contemptuous fury which the intrusion of even a dissyllable would spoil.

In general, however, Pope's monosyllabic lines are not noticeably different from his other lines, though they doubtless contribute to an effect of the easy and (when appropriate) the conversational. In both versions of his letter on prosody, Pope modified his statement with the phrase "unless very artfully managed." There is every reason to believe that he thought himself capable of a management thoroughly artful.[21]

20. In this study I have considered words on the pattern of *even* and *heaven* as monosyllables, because Pope and other eighteenth-century poets freely use them as rimes in poems where no feminine rimes appear unless they themselves be considered so; and because they seem never to be used as dissyllables to occupy a foot. For similar reasons, and because they are used to rime with pure monosyllables, I have considered words on the pattern of *prayer* and *flower* as invariably monosyllabic.
21. It is generally true in Pope that more monosyllables occur in poems involving conversation and in poems of lower style. Thus *Eloisa to Abelard* has 6.32 monosyllables per line; the *First Satire of the Second Book*, 6.33; the

Pope's objection to monosyllabic lines represents one aspect of the eighteenth-century fear of the low, which also expresses itself in use of rhetorical devices, foreign constructions, and "poetic diction." Pope's views in this area are rather liberal. In the Postscript to the *Odyssey* he declares himself opposed to artificial word order, "sudden abruptnesses," "frequent turnings and transpositions"; he objects to the extreme imitations of Milton's style; and it is easy to illustrate out of the Postscript, *The Art of Sinking in Poetry*, and Spence's *Anecdotes* his belief that any one style grows monotonous, and that the style must be varied—high style, middle style, low style—to suit the material.

Nevertheless, Pope uses rhetorical devices constantly. In his works, those devices which occur frequently and generally, and which have an actual, palpable effect upon versification,[22] include exclamation, apostrophe, interrogation, and rhetorical repetition and antithesis. So far as sound effect is concerned, apostrophe, usually exclamatory, may be considered a part of exclamation. The quality of utterance which the two demand is manifestly different from that of simple statement; and the same may be said for interrogation. The three can be illustrated in a single couplet:

Come Abelard! for what hast thou to dread?
The torch of Venus burns not for the dead. (*Eloisa*, 257-258)

The contrast is plain; and if interrogation, for instance,[23] occurs

---

Epistle to Arbuthnot, 6.37. Compare *Windsor-Forest* with 5.63; *Messiah*, 5.64; *An Essay on Criticism*, 5.70; *The Dunciad*, 5.71; *The Rape of the Lock*, 5.92; *An Essay on Man*, 6.00.

Pope used polysyllables (i.e., words of four syllables or more, not reducible to less than four by elision) surprisingly little. The highest count is in *Moral Essays*, I, with occurrence in 7 per cent of the lines. The comparatively high rate in *Eloisa* and *E. on M.* (both 5 per cent) is explainable on the basis of Eloisa's learning (and her repetition of her polysyllabic name!) and the nature of the material in the *Essay*; the figure of only 1 per cent for the four *Pastorals* accords with their "simple" speakers. Polysyllables in Pope occur generally in between 2 per cent and 3 per cent of the lines.

22. Other than inversion for which see below, pp. 21-22. For rhetorical repetition of sound, see below, p. 29. Other rhetorical devices which are especially characteristic of particular poems, such as parenthesis and anticlimax in *The Rape of the Lock*, are examined in the treatment of such poems later in this study.

23. Questions come many times in pairs:
    Is this a dinner? this a Genial room? (*Moral Essays*, IV, 155)

frequently throughout a poem, the tone of the poem must be affected.

Exclamation and interrogation may also affect both the quality and the placement of the caesura:

Without it, proud Versailles! thy glory falls,
(*Moral Essays*, IV, 71)
A Quaker? sly: A Presbyterian? sow'r, (*Moral Essays*, I, 108)
Think we all these are for himself? no more
Than his fine Wife, alas! or finer Whore.
(*Moral Essays*, IV, 11-12)

In some of the serious poems—*Messiah*, for instance—exclamation seems excessive, as if Pope were attempting to substitute for emotion instead of support it; and the tone becomes consequently a little shrill. In fact all three devices—exclamation, interrogation, apostrophe—are best where Pope himself is best: in satire.

Rhetorical repetition is of the very fabric of neoclassic verse. A complete analysis of it in Pope would be a book in itself, and one is confronted with the problem of a reasonable yet adequate limitation. In this study the special devices of repetition referred to regularly by name will be confined to four; not because they are the only four which affect the prosody, but because they are the only four (other than simple parallelism and word repetition) which seem both sufficiently characteristic of Pope and sufficiently distinctive in pattern to be noticed throughout Pope's work by the careful nonprofessional reader. The four are: zeugma, anaphora, chiasmus, and (somewhat separate from the others) antithesis.[24]

The term *zeugma* is used in this study for any instance of one word serving several words, phrases, or clauses,[25] whether the usage is normal:

And is this present, swineherd! of thy hand?
Bring'st thou these vagrants to infest the land? (*Odyssey*, XVII, 450-451)
Canst thou forget that sad, that solemn day,
When victims at yon' altar's foot we lay?
Canst thou forget what tears that moment fell,
When, warm in youth, I bade the world farewell? (*Eloisa*, 107-110)

24. More detailed treatments of rhetorical devices in Pope are to be found elsewhere, e.g., Wimsatt's treatment in *The Verbal Icon* of chiasmus (pp. 162-163) and zeugma (pp. 177-179).

25. This is substantially the first definition in *N.E.D.*

By Day o'ersees them, and by Night protects, (*Messiah*, 52)
or (as in a more limited definition of zeugma) incongruous:

Dost sometimes Counsel take—and sometimes Tea,
(*Rape of the Lock*, III, 8)
Or lose her Heart, or Necklace, at a Ball.
(*Rape of the Lock*, II, 109)

And it is used whether the word which occurs but once appears in the first phrase or clause (as *them*, *take*, and *lose* in the examples just quoted), or in the last:

In Spring the Fields, in Autumn Hills I love. (*Spring*, 77)

Except for the relatively scarce cases of comic incongruity, such usages—they are innumerable in Pope—develop, manifestly, out of the twin desires for balance and condensation.

At times, as in the examples just given from the *Messiah* and *Spring*, zeugma is likely to be somewhat awkward. Such instances grow rarer in Pope's later career, but never wholly disappear; and even though the zeugma becomes smoother, it is still sometimes undesirably apparent:

Nor this a good, nor that a bad we call, (*E. on M.*, II, 55)
Manners with Fortunes, Humours turn with Climes.
(*Moral Essays*, I, 166)

Sometimes, on the other hand, the usage is so natural that it goes completely unnoticed; and it must be remembered that, like the inevitable M. Jourdain and his prose, we all use zeugma without knowing it:

One dy'd in Metaphor, and one in Song,
(*Rape of the Lock*, V, 60)
While Tories call me Whig, and Whigs a Tory.
(*First Satire of the Second Book of Horace*, 68)

Sometimes the device has even a special felicity:

And now a bubble burst, and now a world. (*E. on M.*, I, 90)

But (except, once more, for the instances of incongruity) as a rule only an awkward use of zeugma is sufficiently noticeable to be considered an element of versification separate from the more general parallelism and balance.

Chiasmus is used in this study to refer to any balance in which the elements of the two halves are mirror, rather than identical, images. Thus in this couplet from *An Essay on Man* the two halves of the second line have the same grammatical order and are hence an example of simple balance (ab ab), *not* chiasmus:

Two Principles in human nature reign:
Self-love, to urge, and Reason, to restrain. (II, 53-54)

But in this line from *Windsor-Forest,* the order of grammatical elements in the first part is reversed in the second: and this is chiasmus:

Her Weapons blunted, and extinct her Fires. (418)

This special kind of balance (ab ba) is quite common in Pope. The method occurs in considerable variety:

Sylvia's like Autumn ripe, yet mild as May, (*Spring,* 81)
Directs in council, and in war presides, (*Iliad,* II, 28)
His time a moment, and a point his space, (*E. on M.,* I, 72)
The fewer still you name, you wound the more.
(*First Satire of the Second Book of Horace,* 43)

As related to versification, chiasmus in Pope appears to have two purposes: to provide a suitable rime word (though sometimes, as in *Windsor-Forest*, 418, quoted in the preceding paragraph, the first half-line could be reversed to parallel the second, without disturbing sense or meter, so that the simple balance would provide the same rime), and to gain variety in balance. Also, as with inversion (treated below), chiasmus can emphasize a particular word, or give rime a particularly fine effect. And like zeugma it is especially noticeable when it is awkward.

Anaphora is used in this study to refer to the repetition of a word or words at the beginning of successive, or nearly successive, hemistichs, lines, or couplets. (Pope's other varieties of word repetition are too heterogeneous for useful classification.) Anaphora stands up better than zeugma or chiasmus as a special contribution to verse texture. The repetition of exactly the same word or words in parallel positions means a repetition in sound and either a repetition or a conscious contrast in pitch; and frequent occurrence of such repetitions affects the tone as greatly as repeated exclamation or interrogation. Anaphora by hemistich occurs in

Now warm in love, now with'ring in thy bloom. (*Eloisa,* 37)

By line it occurs in

19

As thick as bees o'er vernal blossoms fly,
As thick as eggs at Ward in Pillory. (*Dunciad*, III, 33-34)

And by couplet it occurs in

For her th'unfading rose of Eden blooms,
And wings of Seraphs shed divine perfumes;
For her the Spouse prepares the bridal ring. (*Eloisa*, 217-219)

It may also be used, though much more rarely, in joining the last line of a couplet to the first of the next:

Which never more shall join its parted Hair,
Which never more its Honours shall renew.
(*Rape of the Lock*, IV, 134-135)

Occasionally too, as in passages in *The Rape of the Lock*, it may occur through a whole series of lines; but this use is plainly artificial (in *The Rape of the Lock*, purposely so); and, as in many of the examples just given, anaphora is more usually an integral part of the thought structure than either zeugma or chiasmus.[26]

Antithesis occurs frequently through all the poems, and has a decided effect upon the tone, since the contrast involves change in pitch, and since antithesis tends to strong caesura and to the neatness of epigram:

To cure thy Lambs, but not to heal thy Heart, (*Summer*, 34)
And she who scorns a Man, must die a Maid,
(*Rape of the Lock*, V, 28)
Born but to die, and reas'ning but to err, (*E. on M.*, II, 10)
Men not afraid of God, afraid of me.
(*Epilogue to the Satires*, II, 209)

Beyond zeugma, chiasmus, anaphora, and antithesis, there are numberless examples in Pope of the balancing of phrase with phrase, clause with clause, hemistich with hemistich, line with line, couplet with couplet;[27] and artful repetition of word or of word arrangement in a never-ending variety:

26. Examples of especially fine integration:
Restore the Lock! she cries; and all around
Restore the Lock! the vaulted Roofs rebound, (*Rape of the Lock*, V, 103-104)
So short a space the light of Heav'n to view!
So short a space! and fill'd with sorrow too! (*Iliad*, I, 544-545)
27. Tillotson treats (pp. 124-130) varieties of balance, especially in connection with variations in the length of balancing elements, and parallels or contrasts of sense and form in the balance.

20

And smooth or rough, with them, is right or wrong,
                                              (*E. on C.*, 338)
Bright as the *Sun*, her Eyes and Gazers strike,
And, *like* the *Sun*, they shine on all *alike*,
                              (*Rape of the Lock*, II, 13-14)
The world forgetting, by the world forgot, (*Eloisa*, 208)
This, all who know me, know; who love me, tell,
              (*First Satire of the Second Book of Horace*, 138)
And Noise and Norton, Brangling and Breval,
Dennis and Dissonance, (*Dunciad*, II, 238-239)
It fled, I follow'd; now in hope, now pain;
It stopt, I stopt; it mov'd, I mov'd again.
                                        (*Dunciad*, IV, 427-428)

As almost any page of Pope will show, these many devices and
methods and turns are combined, intermingled, knotted, loosed, and
resolved, again and again and again. The effect on versification
is very great. Any method involving balance usually at least tends
toward metrical regularity, central caesura, and integrity of line and
couplet; or if it cuts across this normality, then that itself is a
notable effect. On the other hand, too frequent use of the same
rhetorical device can, and in some of Pope's poems does, have an
adverse effect upon tone. At times too, the awkwardness—or conversely the very brilliance—directs the attention away from meaning,
where Pope would have been the first to say it belonged. But the
subtlety and flexibility of Pope's rhetoric increased with the years;
its effect upon meter grew less confining, its support of the sense
more firm.

Inversion is used by Pope, and by neoclassic poets generally, for
at least three purposes, the first two of which are essentially rhetorical: to heighten style; to emphasize a particular word; and to
provide rime. These three types are often almost impossible to
separate with certainty. Even the existence of inversion is not
always definite. Prepositional phrases particularly range rather
widely over a sentence without sounding unnatural. Nevertheless,
there is much unmistakable inversion in Pope. Sometimes it is
clearly for emphasis:

If Hampton-Court these Eyes had never seen,
                                  (*Rape of the Lock*, IV, 150)
Not twice a twelvemonth you appear in Print;
                              (*Epilogue to the Satires*, I, 1)

21

and it can be undeniably so in instances where inversion does not affect rime or meter:

Not on the Cross my eyes were fix'd, but you. *(Eloisa,* 116)

Sometimes, on the other hand, it is merely for rime:

Arise, the Pines a noxious Shade diffuse. *(Winter,* 86)

Yet, in accordance with his views in the Postscript to the *Odyssey,* Pope's inversions are seldom violent; nor are they so frequent as might be supposed. And they grow consistently fewer, especially in the colloquial satires, with their many passages of such completely normal English idiom as this from the *First Satire of the Second Book of Horace*:

> *F.* I'd write no more. *P.* Not write? but then I think,
> And for my Soul I cannot sleep a wink.
> I nod in Company, I wake at Night,
> Fools rush into my Head, and so I write.
> *F.* You could not do a worse thing for your Life.
> Why, if the Nights seem tedious—take a Wife;
> Or rather, truly, if your Point be Rest,
> Lettuce and Cowslip Wine; *Probatum est.*
> But talk with Celsus, Celsus will advise
> Hartshorn, or something that shall close your Eyes.
> Or if you needs must write, write Caesar's Praise:
> You'll gain at least a Knighthood, or the Bays. (11-22)

Even the earlier and the more formal poems have occasional long passages like this one, with not a word out of normal prose order (e.g., *Eloisa,* ll. 249-262; *Essay on Man,* II, 129-144); but they are less likely to be noticed, because less colloquial.

Furthermore, the greatest number by far of Pope's inversions occur in only one line of a couplet, the other line being in normal order; and when the inverted line is the first one—as again is true in most cases—the effect is often to make the rime seem especially neat, giving a turn quite characteristic of Pope.

> But we, brave Britons, Foreign Laws despis'd,
> And kept unconquer'd, and unciviliz'd, *(E. on C.,* 716)
> I shriek, start up, the same sad prospect find,
> And wake to all the griefs I left behind, *(Eloisa,* 247-248)
> That not in Fancy's Maze he wander'd long,
> But stoop'd to Truth, and moraliz'd his song,
> *(Arbuthnot,* 340-341)

22

Blockheads with reason wicked wits abhor,
But fool with fool a barb'rous civil war.
(Dunciad, III, 175-176)

Pope's use of inversion, then, affects his versification mainly in three ways: first, more inversion is likely to make the tone more formal; second, it has an effect upon tone when important words are given important position; third, by its appearance in the first line of a couplet only, it may add aptness and point to the rime with which the couplet closes.

While foreign words and syntax were an accepted method of heightening style in Pope's day, Pope's well-known Latin and French usages are more often one of his methods of gaining succinctness. Three such usages appear fairly often in Pope's verse, and have become somewhat symbolic of foreign diction both in Pope and in neoclassic verse generally. The first of these is the use of *this* and *that* for *the former* and *the latter* (as they are, of course, regularly used in French):

This mourn'd a faithless, that an absent Love, (*Autumn*, 3)
While these they undermine, and those they rend.
(Iliad, XII, 306)

The second is the use, as in Latin and French, of *or* for *either* and *nor* for *neither*:

Not one, or male or female, stay'd behind, (*Odyssey*, IX, 398)
Nor other home nor other care intends. (*Odyssey*, IX, 109)

The third is the suppression of the pronoun following *there are* before a clause beginning with *who, whom,* or *whose*:

There are, who to my Person pay their court, (*Arbuthnot*, 115)
There are to whom my Satire seems too bold,
(First Satire of the Second Book of Horace, 2)
I know there are, to whose presumptuous Thoughts
Those Freer Beauties, ev'n in Them, seem Faults.
(E. on C., 169-170)

In all these un-English usages, the result is condensation—at a minimum, the reduction of a syllable. Otherwise, the effect upon versification is neutral, unless by awkwardness, obscurity, or reappearance to the point of mannerism, such a usage draws attention to itself and away from meaning. And in any case, most of Pope's diction and syntax are native.

23

III

The problems of rime in connection with heroic couplets may be broken down for convenience into four divisions: (1) inaccurate rimes, unstressed rimes, identities; (2) feminine and triple rimes; (3) rime repetition and rime clichés; and (4) violation of normal word order, syntax, or grammar for the sake of rime. Of these, the last has already been examined, and the second may be quickly disposed of. Feminine rimes were unpopular in the eighteenth century, except for the low genres, such as satire. And Pope used such rimes rarely except in his satirical poems, where they appear fairly frequently. Triple rimes were almost unheard of, and do not occur in Pope's verse.

Pope apparently never mentioned the subject of accurate riming; and considering how significant riming is in a tradition of heroic couplets, the subject comes up surprisingly seldom in critical writing generally. Inaccurate rimes are all too frequent in Pope,[28] probably more frequent than in any other important egihteenth-century poets of the heroic couplet tradition; just how frequent is difficult to know, since pronunciations have changed. But clues exist, for example, the fact that the offending word in what seems to us an inaccurate rime is rimed elsewhere in a way which seems to us correct; the fact that some poems, for example *Eloisa to Abelard*, have more rimes which seem inaccurate than other poems;[29] and of course such knowledge as we have of actual pronunciation shifts, as in the cases of *join* and *tea*. Such evidence confirms the impression that Pope was by no means so careful about accurate riming as one might have expected. Even discounting the almost unavoidable inaccuracies with words like *love, God* (which Swift never-

---

28. This discussion of riming might be considered a development of George Sherburn's remarks in *The Best of Pope*, rev. ed. (New York, The Ronald Press Co., 1940), p. xxxi: "In rhyme Pope is much less an artist. . . . Both justness and variety are frequently lacking in his rhymes. He repeats the same rhymes too closely; and even allowing for changes in pronunciation since his day . . . he is too often careless and inexact in his sound identities. It follows that for Pope rhyme is a habit rather than an excellence." But see p. 26, below.

29. Rimes probably inaccurate, not including identities or rimes on syllables not normally bearing a primary accent, occur as follows: *Spring*, 12 per cent of the rimes; *Windsor-Forest*, 10 per cent; *E. on C.*, 10 per cent; *Messiah*, 9 per cent; *Eloisa*, 12 per cent; *Unfortunate Lady*, 5 per cent; *Rape of the Lock*, 8 per cent; *E. on M.*, 13 per cent; *Moral Essays*, I, 8 per cent; *Moral Essays*, II, 9 per cent; *Arbuthnot*, 6 per cent; *First Satire of the Second Book*, 3 per cent; *Augustus*, 8 per cent; *Epilogue*, 7 per cent; *Dunciad*, 4 per cent.

theless objected to as over-frequent and inaccurate),[30] and *heaven*, the number seems large. And Pope's other varieties of carelessness regarding rime are not reassuring. One can find for example, identities:

> Well might I wish, could mortal wish renew
> That strength which once in boiling youth I knew,
> <div align="right">(<i>Iliad</i>, IV, 370-371)</div>

an identity with a lightly-accented syllable:

> Unfinish'd Things, one knows not what to call,
> Their Generation's so equivocal, (*E. on C.*, 42-43)

and even an unquestionably inaccurate identity:

> What future bliss, he gives not thee to know,
> But gives that Hope to be thy blessing now.
> <div align="right">(<i>E. on M.</i>, I, 93-94)[31]</div>

Rimes on unstressed syllables can be noticeable to the point of harshness:

> So shall each hostile name become our own,
> And we too boast our Garth and Addison, (*Dunciad*, II, 139-140)
> In Puns, or Politicks, or Tales, or Lyes,
> Or Spite, or Smut, or Rymes, or Blasphemies.
> <div align="right">(<i>Arbuthnot</i>, 321-322)</div>

The immediate succession of very similar rimes can be annoying, and is rather frequent:

> Some have at first for Wits, then Poets past,
> Turn'd Criticks next, and prov'd plain Fools at last;
> Some neither can for Wits nor Criticks pass,
> As heavy Mules are neither Horse nor Ass, (*E. on C.*, 36-39)
> Now Lakes of liquid Gold, Elysian Scenes,
> And Crystal Domes, and Angels in Machines.
> Unnumber'd Throngs on ev'ry side are seen
> Of Bodies chang'd to various Forms by Spleen,
> <div align="right">(<i>Rape of the Lock</i>, IV, 45-48)</div>

and, worse still:

> This way and that the spreading torrent roars;
> So sweeps the hero thro' the wasted shores.
> Around him wide immense destruction pours,

---

30. Letter to Pope, June 28, 1715 (Sherburn, I, 309).
31. Another example is in *Moral Essays*, I, 110-111.

And earth is deluged with the sanguine showers.
As with autumnal harvests cover'd o'er,
And thick bestrown, lies Ceres' sacred floor. (*Iliad*, XX, 573-578)

Moreover, Pope mentions two faults in the use of rime, and he is guilty of both. First, in his letter on prosody he observes that rime sounds should not be repeated within four to six lines. Second, in *An Essay on Criticism* he makes fun, in a famous passage, of hackneyed rimes. Avoiding almost immediate repetition of the same rime sound ought to be fairly easy and certainly seems desirable; yet it would be difficult to find among his poems one in which Pope is not guilty of such repetition. Even in the earlier poems, when the rule might have been fresh in his mind, Pope repeats his rime sounds; *Autumn* has even the same actual rimes separated by only a single couplet: *move, love* (83-84), *remove, love* (87-88), as does, among others,[32] *Eloisa: away, day* (221-222), *day, away* (225-226); and examples of immediate repetition of the rime *sound* are innumerable. Hackneyed rimes, on the other hand, are harder to avoid. In so overwhelming a number of heroic couplets, it was inevitable that certain rimes should have become commonplace—the *God, abode* combination which Swift mentions, for example. There is little to rime with *death* but *breath*; but, given that deplorable fact about the English language, it would perhaps be wise to allow *death* to turn up as a rime world only very exceptionally. The number of rime combinations which occur too frequently in Pope's poems are far too many.

Yet, as W. K. Wimsatt has pointed out,[33] Pope is capable of consummate artistry in riming, giving his rimes all the desirable qualities of accuracy, variety, inevitability, unexpectedness, and rhetorical point. Many of Pope's most famous couplets—most of the aphorisms in *An Essay on Criticism,* for example—are cases in point. But other couplets from *An Essay on Criticism* may demonstrate more clearly, precisely because they are less familiar:

What woful stuff this Madrigal wou'd be,
In some starv'd Hackny Sonneteer, or me?
But let a Lord once own the happy Lines,
How the Wit brightens! How the Style refines! (418-421)
So much they scorn the Crowd, that if the Throng
By Chance go right, they purposely go wrong. (426-427)

32. E.g., *Epistle to Augustus*, 191-192; 195-196.
33. See n. 2, Introduction, above; also p. 19, above.

The wonder is that, given such superb skill, he should have allowed himself to be so careless.[34] Alliteration, assonance, and other repetition of sounds are among Pope's most frequent and characteristic devices. The variety of uses and the amount of use vary widely from poem to poem to such an extent that discussion of them is best postponed to the examination of those poems—especially *Eloisa to Abelard, Epistle to Arbuthnot, The Dunciad*—where such devices are very important.

We come finally to that chameleon of eighteenth-century prosody, representative meter. Depending upon the critic, or the poet, or the reader, it may involve any element of versification—meter, caesura, word usage, alliteration, and so on—and it may "represent" anything from the most obvious noises to the most complex emotions, and such unrelated phenomena as bulk and temperature. The basic, bare minimum consists of onomatopoetic words, like *buzz, purr, gurgle*; but by "representative meter" Pope clearly means far more than this.[35] And even this minimum has no positive limit,

34. In his letter to Walsh, Pope objected to triplets. They are rare in his work, and what is said in n. 12, above, on Alexandrines, applies here as well.

35. Modern linguists would approach this whole question somewhat differently, being likely to consider any effects not clearly and strictly onomatopoetic (i.e., imitative of sound) to be at least partially subjective, or morphemic, or something in between. Leonard Bloomfield, for example, calls such phonemic sequences as the *fl* of *flip, flop, flutter*, the *sn* of *snore, sniff, snort*, or the *ounce* of *bounce, jounce, pounce*, morphemic (*Language* [New York, Henry Holt and Co., 1933], pp. 242-246). Charles F. Hockett refers to reactions to such sounds as "secondary associations" (and thus apparently subjective reactions to accidental similarities); that is, "the phonemic shape of [a] word sets up reverberations by its acoustic similarity to some other words," especially if the other words have a similar meaning. Thus if we set up a new word *sugg* to mean *beauty* it would seem inappropriate because "its secondary associations with words like *plug, mug, jug, ugly, tug, sag, suck* are too great" (*A Course in Modern Linguistics*, pp. 297-298). For an example of "something in between" see Zellig G. Harris, *Methods in Structural Linguistics* (Chicago, University of Chicago Press, 1951, p. 193). While some of what I describe agrees rather closely with Hockett (see n. 39, below), I have preferred to take an independently empirical approach, without reference to twentieth-century views, for two reasons: (1) I am dealing with the ideas and devices known, or probably known, to Pope, who could not have known twentieth-century theories and concepts; (2) Pope speaks of *representative meter*, by which, in terms of his statements on the subject, the examples he gives, and the techniques he employs, I must take him to refer to *whatever* sounds and movements and patterns help represent the meaning. A larger concept than onomatopoeia, this must be taken to include subjective "representation" (so long as the subjectivity is widely experienced, perhaps through the conditioning effect of tradition) and morphemic "representation." Moreover, linguists seem inclined to grant that, whatever

while certainty recedes farther and farther into the distance as one leaves the simple question of mere words for the more complex devices of alliteration, or run-on lines, or pause; or simple sound correspondence for the more esoteric regions of correspondence in emotion.

Certain real correspondences are of course possible to a line of verse which are not possible to a single word. A line, for example, may describe a sudden stop—and come to a sudden stop; a device which is particularly effective if the stop is at an unexpected place in the line. Moreover, if *hiss* is onomatopoetic, then a line which describes the voice of a serpent and is crowded with *s*'s should be at least equally so. But there is this difference: *hiss* always "represents"; but a sudden stop in an unexpected place may be merely for variety, and a line with numerous *s*'s may have nothing whatever to do with the voice of a serpent. A line describing the halting gait of a cripple may have purposely outlandish meter; but lines that are outlandish metrically may appear quite without intention in the work of a poetaster. The regular practice of a particular poet also makes a difference; if one finds enjambment between couplets in Pope, one seeks a "representative" reason; in Keats' *Endymion*, one most likely does not. Most people would agree that, considering his theories, Pope probably intended the following line to be slow-moving:

And oft look'd back, slow-moving o'er the strand. (*Iliad*, I, 453)

But they may or may not agree that it *is* slow-moving. On the other hand, the following line seems to me to "represent" not swiftness but the rocking, "bounding" motion which is the type of motion being described:

Above the bounding billows swift they flew. (*Iliad*, I, 628)

This time, I imagine, many people would doubt that such an effect was intended, much less achieved, especially since Pope's recorded statements offer no direct evidence that he believed such an effect possible, as they do regarding speed or its lack. All I can do, there-

---

they call such phenomena, the linguistically untrained reader (such as Pope!) will assume them to be representational or even onomatopoetic. See, for example, Bloomfield, p. 156 ("to the speaker it seems as if the sounds were especially suited to the meaning"); and Charlton Laird, *The Miracle of Language* (Cleveland, World Publishing Co., 1953, p. 73).

fore, is to point out the three successive *b*'s and the trochaic effect of *bounding billows* and say (rather helplessly) that to me the rocking motion is there; that the elements I have indicated seem to me to put it there; and that such techniques as alliteration in so careful a poet as Pope are not, generally speaking, random.[36] But to one who (quite legitimately) finds, even after it is suggested to him, no correspondence between the significance of the word *bounding* and the movement of the line, I should have proved exactly nothing. After all, a good deal of the correspondence between sound and sense in poetry is conventional. We have come to accept back vowels as an element in solemnity or gloom, *r*'s for roughness, difficult pronunciation for difficult movement, voiced continuants for smoothness, and so on. These are conventions. Nothing is inherently gloomy about the *o* of *solemn* or the *oo* of *doom*, nor would we find them so in *mollycoddle* or *food*. But we have come to accept the view that *if the sense is mournful*, back vowels help emphasize it. We prefer the effect to be subtle; but we should feel uncomfortable at a line expressive of gloom in which the dominant sounds were short front vowels and unvoiced stopped consonants.

There is, of course, another sort of representation which is more rhetorical in nature. Pope's two commonest uses of alliteration fall into this category: parallel alliteration reinforcing parallel sense; alliteration of adjective and substantive reinforcing the union of the two. Existence of this sort of representative meter is not especially disputed or disputable; and it is probably this sort which eighteenth-century critics sometimes had in mind when they reiterated their pleas for a correspondence of sound and sense.

Pope himself stated strongly in his letter on prosody that verse should imitate sound and motion, and can do it well:

> It is not enough that nothing offends the ear . . . in describing a gliding stream, the numbers should run easy and flowing; in describing a rough torrent or deluge, sonorous and swelling; and so of the rest. . . .
> This, I think, is what very few observe in practice, and is undoubtedly of wonderful force in printing the image on the reader.

36. I. A. Richards gives very similar examples of lines relating alliteration and movement to a description of movement (*Principles of Literary Criticism*, pp. 144-145).

The famous passage in *An Essay on Criticism* (ll. 364-373) is a versification of this almost exactly, except that it goes on (ll. 374-383) to praise emotional correspondence as well. In his letter Pope had mentioned Homer and Virgil as pre-eminently successful practitioners of representation; and in his later essays on Homer in connection with his translations, he went even farther, praising both poets for their skill in matching sound to sense, in terms indicating that he meant more than mere general correspondence, for example:

> Thus his [Homer's] measures, instead of being fetters to his sense, were always in readiness to run along with the warmth of his rapture, and even to give a farther representation of his notions, in the correspondence of the sounds to what they signified.[37]

In view of such statements, it is not surprising that Pope's practice could easily be used as a manual of methods of successful representation. Many of his wonderfully skillful displays of representative meter are famous: the close of *The Dunciad*, the portrait of Sporus in *Epistle to Dr. Arbuthnot*, various passages in *The Rape of the Lock*. Pope's representation in its simplest form depends heavily on onomatopoetic words:

> Th'impatient weapon whizzes on the wing;
> Sounds the tough horn, and twangs the quiv'ring string.
> (*Iliad*, IV, 156-157)

But he imitates movement, or movement and sound, more often than sound alone; and this requires more complex means:

> As torrents roll, increas'd by numerous rills,
> With rage impetuous down their echoing hills;
> Rush to the vales, and, pour'd along the plain,
> Roar thro' a thousand channels to the main. (*Iliad*, IV, 516-519)

Here the impression of swift, loud movement is created by the many *r*'s, the back vowels, the avoidance of consonant clusters and consequent ease of pronunciation, the lack of spondees, the several light feet, the several trisyllables, the initial trochees, the late caesura in the last line. Slow, smooth motion can be equally well represented:

> In a soft, silver Stream dissolv'd away. (*Windsor-Forest*, 204)

37. Preface to the *Iliad*, *Complete Poetical Works*, p. 254.

And so can more specialized motions, such as shrinking or contraction:

> Or Alom-Stypticks with contracting Power
> Shrink his thin Essence like a rivell'd Flower.
> *(Rape of the Lock,* II, 131-132)

Here, among the elements contributing to the effect are the "dry" sound of the many unvoiced stops (two *p*'s, three *k*-sounds, four *t*'s) in the first line, especially in juxtaposition—*pt* and *ct*, both heavily accented; the contrasting "thin" continuants, mostly dental (*sh, s, n*) in the second line; and in both lines the short front vowels, representative of littleness.

Short front vowels can equally well represent a mental or emotional rather than a physical littleness:

> Thron'd in the Centre of his thin designs;
> Proud of a vast Extent of flimzy lines. *(Arbuthnot,* 93-94)

In this passage, Pope applies to versification his favorite humorous device of anticlimax, allowing the resonant back vowels in the first half of each line *(throned, proud, vast)* to lapse into a "flimsy" mass of short *e*'s and *i*'s.

But as a confused littleness can be represented, so can a confused bigness:

> The gath'ring number, as it moves along,
> Involves a vast involuntary throng. *(Dunciad,* IV, 81-82)

Here the repeated *v*'s and *l*'s, the open back vowels, and the polysyllable are as effective as they are reminiscent of Milton.

Types of feet may be used for representation. The sense of the word *equal* is matched by the regular iambics in

> And urg'd the rest by equal Steps to rise. *(E. on C.,* 97)

The opportunity to linger over the second foot in the following line, effected by the spondee and the long vowels and the nasal continuants, reinforces the idea of length and of funereal slowness:

> While the long fun'rals blacken all the way.
> *(Unfortunate Lady,* 40)

And very occasionally, as I have already noticed, real violence is done to the iambic pattern for the sake of representation:

> Jumping, high o'er the shrubs of the rough ground,

31

Rattle the clatt'ring cars, and the shock'd axles bound.

(*Iliad*, XXIII, 142-143)

Here, where jumping and rattling and jerky movement are described, the first line has only one iambic foot, and in the second line (an Alexandrine), even if *clatt'ring* is accepted as a dissyllable, there are only three iambic feet out of six.

The use of difficult pronunciation to represent difficult physical exertion appears again and again, for example:

Then fierce Tydides stoops; and, from the fields
Heav'd with vast force, a rocky fragment wields.

(*Iliad*, V, 369-370)

Enjambment may have a representative purpose, often, as in the following couplet, in combination with unusual caesura:

Which,/without passing thro' the Judgment,/gains
The Heart,/and all its End at once attains. (*E. on C.*, 156-157)

Unusual caesura may be used for climax:

To help me thro' this long Disease,/my Life, (*Arbuthnot*, 132)

or for anticlimax:

The Mighty Mother, and her Son who brings
The Smithfield Muses to the ear of Kings,
I sing./ (*Dunciad*, I, 1-3)

And after all it is in humor that Pope's skill is greatest and most characteristic.[38] One knows of no one else who can achieve quite such effects as the brilliantly risible

As when a dab-chick waddles thro' the copse. (*Dunciad*, II, 63)

There are more difficult cases. One feels a representative quality in such a couplet as

Weak, foolish man! will Heav'n reward us there
With the same trash mad mortals wish for here?

(*E. on M.*, IV, 173-174)

In this and many other instances, Pope gains his effect in part by analyzing his principal, usually unpleasant, word or words—in this case, *trash*—and repeating its principal elements elsewhere in the lines. Here the *sh* is repeated in *foolish* and *wish*, and the short *a*

38. Cf. Tillotson, p. 121.

in *man* and *mad*, thus accounting for most of the key words. To this he adds an (almost surely purposely) obvious and hence ill-sounding alliteration (*weak, will, with, wish; man, mad, mortal*). And he thus succeeds in transmitting the distinct impression that the lines themselves have an unpleasant texture to match their meaning.[39] Another instance of this is:

In the fat Age of Pleasure, Wealth, and Ease,
Sprung the rank Weed, and thriv'd with large Increase.

(E. on C., 534-535)[40]

Several unpleasant ideas appear in the first line: "fat age," and (in context) "pleasure" and "ease." And the short *a* of *fat* is repeated in *rank*; the soft *g* of *age* is repeated in *large* (and there is the closely related *s* of *pleasure*); the short *e* of *pleasure* appears again in *wealth*; and the long *e* of *ease* in *weed* and *increase*. In addition, there are the alliteration of *wealth* and *weed;* and the ugly contrast of the many smooth sounds (voiced continuants, like the *s* in *pleasure* and the *v* in *thriv'd*; drawn-out vowels, like the *i* in *thriv'd* and the *a* in *large*) with the evil luxuriance of the meaning. Smoothness plus corruption equal decadence; and decadence is precisely the effect obtained in these lines. Such a combination of techniques accounts for the ugliness of many unpleasant passages in the *Epistle to Arbuthnot, The Dunciad,* and numerous other poems.

Pope's range in representative meter was wide. One of the major purposes in any poem-by-poem analysis of his prosody must be to show the astonishing variety and astonishingly consistent effectiveness of his "representative" effects.

39. This technique seems to be close to what Hockett refers to as "secondary association." See n. 35, above.
40. The apparent borrowing from Shakespeare shows only that Shakespeare came close to the same technique:
And duller shouldst thou be than the fat weed
That rots itself in ease on Lethe wharf. (*Hamlet,* I, v, 32-33)

2. EARLY AND ROMANTIC

I

The heroic couplet as Pope uses it in the *Pastorals* and *Windsor-Forest* and the other early poems is already a fine instrument, capable of fairly subtle modulation. Yet quite naturally, the *Pastorals* come nearer in spirit to the strict prosodic rules of Pope's letter, and have fewer exceptions, than almost any other of his poems. They depart comparatively seldom, for example—though they do depart—from the caesura established as orthodox in his letter,[1] that following the fourth, fifth, or sixth syllable. Such a passage as the following from *Autumn* is typical:

Resound ye Hills, resound my mournful Lay!	4
Beneath yon Poplar oft we past the Day:	5
Oft on the Rind I carv'd her Am'rous Vows,	4
While She with Garlands hung the bending Boughs:	5
The Garlands fade, the Vows are worn away;	4
So dies her Love, and so my Hopes decay. (65-70)	4

Pope displays this preference also in *Windsor-Forest* and the *Messiah*; and while orthodox caesuras diminish fairly steadily thereafter, the more formal poems are always likely to have more of them. But in no poem later than *Spring* is the preference for the fourth-place caesura so strong, occurring in more than half the lines; and it is very high in the other *Pastorals* as well. This emphasis upon the fourth-place caesura has probably a good deal to do with the *Pastorals'* artificial tone, though the *Pastorals* are also unusual in having more second-place caesuras than sixth—and indeed for having more caesuras in the first half of the line than any later poems examined in this study.

But while Pope obviously stayed closer to the rules in the *Pastorals* than he did later, he was already able to depart from them with notable skill, not merely for variety, but for calculated effect, as for instance:

Thro' Rocks and Caves/ the Name of Delia sounds,
Delia,/each Cave and ecchoing Rock rebounds, (*Autumn*, 49-50)

---

1. The rule for not more than three successive caesuras is also, more surprisingly, broken; see pp. 6-7 and n. 6, Chapter I, above.

34

The Moon,/serene in Glory,/mounts the Sky, (*Winter*, 6)
and the truly excellent

No more the mounting Larks,/ while Daphne sings,
Shall/list'ning in mid Air/suspend their Wings. (*Winter*, 53-54)

The most important difference in caesura between the *Pastorals*
and *Windsor-Forest* is the significant increase in sixth-place caesuras,
and *Windsor-Forest* is the significant increase in sixth-place caesuras

Earth's distant Ends our Glory shall behold,	4
And the new World launch forth to seek the Old.	6
Then Ships of uncouth Form shall stem the Tyde,	6
And Feather'd People crowd my wealthy Side,	5
And naked Youths and painted Chiefs admire	4
Our Speech, our Colour, and our strange Attire!	2-5
Oh stretch thy Reign, fair Peace! from Shore to Shore,	6
Till Conquest cease, and Slav'ry be no more:	4
Till the freed Indians in their native Groves	5
Reap their own Fruits, and woo their Sable Loves,	4
Peru once more a Race of Kings behold,	4
And other Mexico's be roof'd with Gold. (401-412)	6

Throughout his career, Pope used this increase in the sixth-place
caesura as one method of attaining dignity, solemnity, or mag-
nificence: in the *Messiah*; in the powerful opening eighteen lines
of *An Essay on Man*, Epistle II; in the story of Sir Balaam in the
third *Moral Essay*; in the close of *The Dunciad*. Thus while a
certain tendency may be discerned on the basis of time only—the
sixth-place caesura is never again so rare as in the *Pastorals*—the
principal cause of variation here, as elsewhere in Pope's prosody,
is the matching of sound to sense. Sixth-place caesuras, as Johnson
was to point out, are as a type majestic. A few of them are always
essential for variety; but they should occur more frequently only
when an actual majesty or solemnity of thought is to be clothed in
verse suitable to it.

Both the *Pastorals* and *Windsor-Forest* are close to rule regarding
meter. Here even the initial trochee, always a common Pope variant, is scarcer than in any later important poem except the *Messiah*.[2] Medial trochees are, as always, rare, but Pope already knew

2. In the *Pastorals*, the occurrence is about one line in ten; in *The Rape of
the Lock*, about one in five; in the *First Satire of the Second Book of Horace*,
about one in four.

35

how to employ this variant for special effect:

And the fleet Shades glide o'er the dusky Green, (*Autumn*, 64)

See! the bold Youth strain up the threatning Steep.

(*Windsor-Forest*, 155)

The *Pastorals* are especially regular, the measures tripping lightly along with little interruption of any sort. This is perhaps as it should be in the pastoral, so long as regularity does not mean monotony; and in a form which is itself so artificial and filled with set speeches, a style either loose or abrupt, either colloquial or impassioned, would seem incongruous. If the pastoral is used as a vehicle for deep emotion as it is by Milton or Matthew Arnold, then one expects a fuller, more open style. But while Pope's pastorals are not shallow—it is surprising how much real feeling hides beneath the decorousness of the form—they are nevertheless intended principally for light connoisseur amusement, and a more complex metrical variety would be unsuitable.

There is nothing very remarkable about the use of line and couplet in the *Pastorals*. Closed couplets occur more frequently, especially in the portions intended as songs, than was Pope's later custom; and long series of interrelated couplets are prevented by the alternation of singers in the contest in *Spring* and by the refrains in *Autumn* and *Winter*. The very fact of song makes a division into smaller and more regular word-groups desirable. An occasional variation occurs, however, of a type not much found elsewhere in Pope:

> In Spring the Fields, in Autumn Hills I love,
> At Morn the Plains, at Noon the shady Grove;
> But Delia always,   (*Spring*, 77-79)
> Ye shady Beeches, and ye cooling Streams,
> Defence from Phoebus', not from Cupid's Beams;
> To you I mourn.   (*Summer*, 13-15)[3]

The same pattern appears in *Windsor-Forest*.[4] And *Windsor-*

---

3. The semicolons preventing normal enjambment between the second and third lines in each of these quotations are abnormal both grammatically and in Pope's practice, see n. 16, Chapter I, above. The grammatically impossible punctuation of the 1st edition may in this case represent Pope's youthful hesitation to break the couplet pattern. As the two subsequent quotations (see note 4) from *Windsor-Forest* show, he soon lost his hesitancy.

4. E.g., ll. 1-3 and 349-351. See also *Messiah*, ll. 3-5.

Forest, lacking refrains or songs and containing narrative, fuller description, and more complex thought sequences, is naturally freer than the *Pastorals* in the use of open couplets. Open series of at least three or four couplets are common, and there is one instance of eight (ll. 241-256).[5] Strong enjambment within the couplet is scarce, but it does occur in both the *Pastorals* (e.g., *Winter*, ll. 65-66) and *Windsor-Forest* (e.g., ll. 91-92).

Song, alternation of speakers, and use of refrains, as well as the earliness of the work are some of the reasons for the general integrity of line and couplet in the *Pastorals*. The almost uninterrupted flow of the various rhetorical devices of repetition and antithesis is yet another.[6] This rhetoric is a source of both strength and weakness in the *Pastorals*: strength, because, if lines and couplets *are* to be units, rhetorical patterning helps to hold them together, and because word play is a natural and acceptable element in love songs; weakness, because Pope had not yet learned so to control and limit his rhetoric as to point up the meaning rather than call attention to itself. In *Spring*, for example, one finds many instances of simple parallelism, often with rhetorical alliteration:

You, that too Wise for *P*ride, too *G*ood for *P*ow'r; (7)

zeugma:

Two Swains, whom Love kept wakeful, and the Muse; (18)

chiasmus, again with alliteration:

*F*resh as the Morn, and as the Season *f*air; (20)

anaphora:

Why sit we mute, when early Linnets sing,
When warbling Philomel salutes the Spring?
Why sit we sad, when Phosphor shines so clear,
And lavish Nature paints the Purple Year? (25-28)

and antithesis:

She runs, but hopes she does not run unseen. (58)

5. Syntactically. The punctuation of the 1st edition again obscures, and distorts, the grammar.
6. See also Tw., I, 54-55, and Tillotson, pp. 124-131. Other rhetorical devices, such as apostrophe, exclamation, interrogation, and rhetorical inversion, are also very frequent; but since they do not involve repetition and balance, they do not concern the present argument.

37

But this list is not complete: there is, in one form or another, constant very neat rhetorical patterning of words, phrases, and clauses, constant rhetorical balance of line with line, stanza with stanza. Zeugma and anaphora are especially frequent; and the former can be very graceful:

If Delia smile, the Flow'rs begin to spring,
The Skies to brighten, and the Birds to sing. (71-72)

But it can also be very awkward:

In Spring the Fields, in Autumn Hills I love. (77)

Almost every line in *Spring* is a part, too often obviously, of such balance.

The other three *Pastorals* are not so noticeably rhetorical as *Spring*, partly because they do not consist of alternate singing, with each singer trying to cap the other. The rhetorical repetition is more varied, too, and somewhat more subtle, for example, the famous lines from *Summer*:

Where-e'er you walk, cool Gales shall fan the Glade,
Trees, where you sit, shall crowd into a Shade,
Where-e'er you tread, the blushing Flow'rs shall rise,
And all things flourish where you turn your Eyes. (73-76)

Pope uses rhetorical repetition less obviously in *Windsor-Forest* than in the *Pastorals*. Even when the word play is noticeable, as in the rhetorical alliteration of

The lonely Lords of empty Wilds and Woods, (48)

it has as a rule a felicity which is its own excuse. As might be expected, antithesis occurs far more frequently than in the *Pastorals*:

And where, tho' all things differ, all agree, (16)
But while the Subject starv'd, the Beast was fed. (60)

On the whole, Pope here integrates his rhetoric far better than in the *Pastorals*, and while he certainly employs such characteristic devices as zeugma and chiasmus, they are less frequent and much less apparent. The rhetoric of the later and in some ways technically finer *Eloisa to Abelard* is much more obvious than that of *Windsor-Forest*.

Pope keeps his language in the *Pastorals* appropriately simple. They and *Windsor-Forest* alike have fewer polysyllabic words proportionately than any other of his major poems.[7] Since the *Pastorals* combine formality and simplicity, it is not surprising that they are almost exactly average in monosyllables per line. Since *Winter* is an elegy, and hence of greatest dignity, it is not surprising that it has the fewest monosyllables of the four. And since *Windsor-Forest* is more formal and intellectual than the *Pastorals*, it is not surprising that its monosyllable rate is much lower than the average of theirs.[8] But considering how much space is devoted to description, the *Pastorals* are also remarkably abundant in verbs[9]— an excellent sign that Pope learned much of his trade very early. On the other hand, both the *Pastorals* and *Windsor-Forest* are high in adjectives; and however effective the individual epithets may be, entirely too many two-syllable epithets are used at least partly to fill out the decasyllabic pattern, for example:

She saw her Sons with (purple) Deaths expire,
Her sacred Domes involv'd in (rolling) Fire,
A (dreadful) Series of Intestine Wars, (*Windsor-Forest*, 323-325)
For her, the Flocks refuse their (verdant) Food,
The thirsty Heifers shun the (gliding) Flood.
The silver Swans her (hapless) Fate bemoan, (Winter, 37-39)

and the almost unforgivable

The gulphy Lee his sedgy Tresses rears. (*Windsor-Forest*, 346)

But again these are lapses which Pope would not have permitted himself later; and again one finds beside them truly excellent use of the same method:

And makes his trembling Slaves the Royal Game.
(*Windsor-Forest*, 64)

Other than for simple parallelism[10] and—especially in *Windsor-*

7. One each in *Spring, Summer*, and *Winter*, none in *Autumn*. They occur in 1 per cent of the lines in *Windsor-Forest*. See n. 21, Chapter I, above.
8. *Pastorals*, 5.97 monosyllables per line; *Winter*, 5.50; *Windsor-Forest*, 5.63. On the other hand, the *Pastorals* contain only five monosyllabic lines, or about 1 per cent; *Windsor-Forest*, slightly more.
9. *Spring* has 1.34 verbs per line. Verbs in Pope range from 1.01 per line in *The Dunciad* to 1.44 in *Epilogue to the Satires*. *Spring* is high. (The verb count includes participles when their use is clearly more verbal than adjectival; infinitives; and auxiliaries other than the perfect, emphatic, continuous, future, passive, and conditional, which are included only if they appear in a separate line from the main verb.)
10. Sometimes not so simple:

Forest—to emphasize the union of substantive and adjective, Pope uses alliteration (and other consonant patterning) in these poems mainly to heighten passages of rich description:

Now *b*right Arcturus *g*lads the teeming *G*rain,
Now *G*olden *F*ruits on loaded *B*ranches shine,
And *g*rateful *C*lusters swell with *f*loods of Wine;
Now *b*lushing *B*erries paint the yellow Grove, (*Autumn*, 72-75)
Or under *S*outhern *S*kies exalt their *S*ails,
Led by new *S*tars, and *b*orn by *s*picy Gales!
For me the *B*alm shall *b*leed, and Amber flow,
The Coral *r*edden, and the *R*uby glow. (*Windsor-Forest*, 391-394)

Assonance is often used in the same way:

O'er *G*olden Sands let rich Pact*o*lus flow, (*Spring*, 61)
His P*u*rple Crest, and Scarlet-c*i*rcled Eyes, (*Windsor-Forest*, 116)
Where clearer Flames glow round the fr*o*zen P*o*le.
(*Windsor-Forest*, 390)

The finest example of assonance in *Windsor-Forest*, however, is effective far beyond mere adornment. The meaning itself is intensified by the beautiful interplay of closely related back vowels (not all of them actually assonantal) in

With sl*au*ght'ring G*u*ns th '*u*nweary'd F*ow*ler r*o*ves,
When Frosts have whiten'd *a*ll the naked Groves;
Where D*o*ves in Fl*o*cks the leafless Trees *o*'ershade,
And lonely W*oo*dcocks h*au*nt the w*a*try Glade. (125-128)

The assonance of "leafless trees" is a beautiful contrast to the main theme; the long *a* rime of the second couplet is finely anticipated in "naked." Pope seldom employed his skill for a purpose quite like this, and when he did he rarely surpassed the workmanship here displayed.

Even more complex vowel (and consonant) patterning occurs in the *Pastorals*, but without the delicate music and close support of meaning which makes the *Windsor-Forest* passage so effective:

M*e* gentle D*e*lia b*e*ckons from the Pl*ai*n,
$$\underset{e}{-}\ \underset{e}{\smile}\ \underset{e}{-}\ \underset{e}{\smile}\ \underset{a}{-}$$

If D*e*lia smile, the Flow'rs begin to *s*pring,
The *S*kies to *b*righten, and the *B*irds to *s*ing. (*Spring*, 71-72)

Then hid in Shades, *eludes* her *eager* Swain;

     ⌣ – – – –
     e a e e a

But f*ei*gns a Laugh, to *see* m*e* search around, *(Spring, 53-55)*

    – – –
    a e e

*N*ow *r*ise, and ha*st*e *to* yon*der* Wood*b*i*n*e *B*ow'*r*s,

   n r s t t n d r d b n b r

A *soft Retreat* from *sudden* vernal Show'*rs.*

   s t r t r t r s d n r n r *(Spring, 97-98)*

This sort of purely ornamental complexity is rare in Pope except in the descriptive poetry up to 1717. It reaches its height in *Eloisa to Abelard.*

On the other hand, simpler patterns of internal consonants (particularly *l, m, n, and r*) appear quite effectively in both the *Pastorals* and *Windsor-Forest*:

Let Ver*n*al Ai*r*s th*ro*' t*r*emb*l*ing Osie*r*s p*l*ay, *(Spring, 5)*
The vivid Gree*n* his shi*n*ing P*l*u*m*es u*nf*o*l*d;
His pai*n*ted Wi*n*gs, and Breast that f*lam*es with Go*l*d.

         (Windsor-Forest, 117-118)

Nevertheless in the *Pastorals* even the simplest sound repetition may unpleasantly call attention to itself:

Nor *bl*ush to sport on Windsor's *bl*issful Plains, (Spring, 2)
Em*b*race my Love, and *b*ind my *B*rows with *B*ays, *(Summer, 38)*

and particularly the purposeless hissing of

Ble*st* Swain*s*, whose Nymph*s* in ev'ry Grace e*x*cell;
Ble*st* Nymph*s*, who*s*e *S*wain*s* those Grace*s s*ing *so* well!

         (Spring, 95-96)

Windsor-Forest is freer from such lapses, largely because even the more obvious sound repetition is likely to have a purpose in "representing" or unifying prominent ideas:

But when the *tainted Ga*les the *Ga*me be*tr*ay, (101)
To Plains with well-*breath*'d *Bea*gles we repair, (121)
They fall, and *l*eave their *l*ittle *L*ives in Air. (134)

But the obvious and hence self-defeating use of sound repetition was a fault of which Pope was more than occasionally guilty, at least until after those poems collected in 1717.

Many of the lines already quoted from the *Pastorals* and *Windsor-Forest* demonstrate that the young Pope already knew much about representative meter. He knew, abundantly well, for example, what could be done with the caesura:

> Oft as the mounting Larks their Notes prepare,
> They fall,/and leave their little Lives in Air.
> (Windsor-Forest, 133-134)

He knew what could be done with the apparent trochee:

> Now *fainting, sinking*, pale, the Nymph appears;
> (Windsor-Forest, 191)

and (though not yet extensively) with the real:

> Flutters in Blood, and panting beats the Ground.
> (Windsor-Forest, 114)

He could run his verse swift and open through several lines when the sense seemed to need it:

> It chanc'd, as eager of the Chace the Maid
> Beyond the Forest's verdant Limits stray'd,
> Pan saw and lov'd, and burning with Desire
> Pursu'd her Flight. (*Windsor-Forest*, 181-184)

Already in *Winter*, he was capable of a gradual rising and opening, from a quiet, almost hesitant movement to a full roaring sweep:

> Her Fate is whisper'd by the gentle Breeze,
> And told in Sighs to all the trembling Trees;
> The trembling Trees, in ev'ry Plain and Wood,
> Her Fate remurmur to the silver Flood;
> The silver Flood, so lately calm, appears
> Swell'd with new Passion, and o'erflows with Tears;
> The Wind and Trees and Floods her Death deplore,
> Daphne, our Grief! our Glory now no more! (61-68)

In addition to the change in the quality of vowels and consonants from first to last in this passage, and the change in caesural value, and the increase in number of heavy beats per line; and in addition to the enjambment between lines 65 and 66, which hastens the flow, line 67, a type found rarely in Pope, increases both speed and emphasis because all the feet are true iambs and there is almost no pause.[11]

An even more notable example of shift in tone, and perhaps

---

11. That is, each iamb consists either of one single dissyllabic word or of two monosyllabic words. Contrast the third line, in which the *meter* is iambic, but words must be divided to form the iambs.

the most notable single effect in the whole of these early poems, is the close of *Windsor-Forest*. Like Milton in *Lycidas*, Pope abandons emotional fire and heat for a quiet conclusion:

Here cease thy flight.... (423)

The change is sudden. The contrast is tremendous. And one realizes something new about the quality of quiet. Left behind is the thunder—perhaps, it must be admitted, a thunder perilously close to bathos—of such lines as

Exil'd by Thee from Earth to deepest Hell,
In Brazen Bonds shall barb'rous Discord dwell:
Gigantick Pride, pale Terror, gloomy Care,
And mad Ambition, shall attend her there. (413-416)

The sound and the fury are replaced by the peaceful tenor of

My humble Muse, in unambitious Strains,
Paints the green Forests and the flow'ry Plains,
Where Peace descending bids her Olives spring,
And scatters Blessings from her Dove-like Wing. (427-430)

And so on. No matter that Pope was following Milton—and these are not the only echoes of Milton in *Windsor-Forest*—he has achieved a significant effect of his own. If the effect seems to be too much like that in Mendelssohn's *Spring Song*, it is probably because the technique is superior to the material.

The *Pastorals* and *Windsor-Forest* are, to be sure, limited in scope; but so far as they go, they show clearly the promise which Pope's later work was to fulfill. If one cannot know from them that Pope will use sound patterns consummately well to intensify the emotion of disgust as he does in *The Dunciad*, one may at least expect that when so young a poet has already so fine (if not consistent) a touch with alliteration and assonance, a brilliant, sustained, and superbly flexible use of those techniques will be forthcoming. If one cannot anticipate from them the beautiful conversational tone of passages in the later satires, one may guess that a youth with the ideal of correctness ringing in his ears who can yet—if so far only occasionally—break rules with skill and purpose, will make of his chosen verse form a very cunning instrument. The *Pastorals* and *Windsor-Forest* have their depths as well as their eminences; and in them few rules are lightly broken. It could not be otherwise. But few poets anywhere ever came forth into the world with so many of their characteristic excellences already on display for all who read to see and for at least the unenvious to admire.

II

In general metrical technique, the *Messiah* rather closely resembles *Windsor-Forest*: in orthodox caesuras (at a high rate among Pope's poems), in use of the initial trochee (low), in proportion of monosyllables and of monosyllabic lines (low). Distinctly an early poem, its principal variation from the metrical pattern of the other early poems lies in its increase in caesuras in the latter half of the line and particularly the sixth-place caesura; a variation to be expected of a poem attempting to achieve sublimity. Also it has far more elision by apocope than either *Windsor-Forest* or the *Pastorals*—more proportionately than any other major poem. (Pope clearly thought apocope more suitable to formal poems.) In its brief 108 lines the *Messiah* has several series of open couplets (e.g., ll. 49-56). While there is much balance of phrase against phrase, clause against clause, and line against line, the method is not so insistent as in the *Pastorals* (or *Eloisa*),[12] and the more complex devices of rhetorical repetition are, except for a rather simple zeugma, infrequent. On the other hand, Pope here depends heavily on apostrophe and exclamation as means—not entirely successful means—of heightening, which anticipates *Eloisa*:

> See spicy Clouds from lowly Saron rise,
> And Carmel's flow'ry Top perfumes the Skies!
> Hark! a glad Voice the lonely Desert chears:
> Prepare the Way! a God, a God appears. (27-30)

Yet the descriptions which in *Windsor-Forest* and in *Eloisa* inspire him to employ elaborate alliteration, assonance, and other sound patterning, lapse in the *Messiah* to mere dry lists with comparatively little attempt at prosodic adornment:

> And Starts, amidst the thirsty Wilds, to hear
> New Falls of Water murm'ring in his Ear:
> On rifted Rocks, the Dragon's late Abodes,
> The green Reed trembles, and the Bulrush nods.
> Waste sandy Vallies, once perplex'd with Thorn,
> The spiry Firr and shapely Box adorn;
> To leaf-less Shrubs the flow'ring Palms succeed,

12. See Tw., I, 104.

And od'rous Myrtle to the noisome Weed.
The Lambs with Wolves shall graze the verdant Mead,
And Boys in flow'ry Bands the Tyger lead;
The Steer and Lion at one Crib shall meet;
And harmless Serpents lick the Pilgrim's Feet. (69-80)

The only alliteration is the minor example in line 71, the only noticeable assonance in lines 72, 73, and 75; and it is astonishing to find Pope describing a waterfall without any attempt at representative meter. One line only,

The crested Basilisk and speckled Snake, (82)

has the life that Pope usually gives to his descriptions in other poems; and even this line is a reminder that elsewhere in the *Messiah* the two-syllable epithet is likely to be as obvious as it is in *Windsor-Forest* and the *Pastorals*.[13]

Indeed in the whole of the *Messiah* Pope makes the least possible use of special representative technique, whether of meter or of caesura or of repetition of sound. But the Alexandrine, fittingly, appears several times and well.[14] The language of Scripture does sometimes gain exciting statement:

The Dumb shall sing, the Lame his Crutch foregoe,
And leap exulting like the bounding Roe. (43-44)

There are, not unexpectedly, fine hints of Milton:

And on the sightless Eye-ball pour the Day. (40)

And the last twenty-four lines of the poem, beginning

Rise, crown'd with Light, Imperial Salem rise! (85)

do rise to a reality of fervor and splendor. That they do this without going beyond the spareness of prosodic technique characteristic of the entire poem may be evidence that Pope felt this spareness to be most appropriate to Scriptural materials. But

13. Pope's use of epithets, and his descriptions generally, in the *Messiah* are defended in Tw., I, 105-106, and by other critics; but the defense seems to be on grounds of literary theory rather than prosodic, or even poetic effect. To demonstrate that the poem suited Pope's taste and that of his period is worthwhile, but does not prove that the same techniques remain effective today; rather, it is to demonstrate that the Augustan techniques of (for example) mock-epic have lasted better than those of pastoral or—and Tw. compares Pope's use of Isaiah to his use of Homer—epic. No one would feel impelled to a historical defense of *The Rape of the Lock*.
14. See Tw., I, 107.

apostrophe and exclamation, elsewhere in the poem used to excess and superimposed, are here sufficient and organic; the images are grand, the language almost equally so; the regularity of meter is a virtue; the one instance of overflowing the couplet and of enjambment is perfectly suitable, cuts across the pattern just enough, a disciplined excess.[15] The final Alexandrine brings the passage to a triumphant and exalted close. These twenty-four lines are almost beyond analysis, because there is almost nothing to analyze. Emotion, which in the earlier passages had been beaten up hill with the stick of exclamation, now suddenly strides forth free and strong. The passage is like nothing else in Pope; it reveals an aspect of his genius seen nowhere else in his entire poetical career.

III

Eloisa to Abelard and the *Elegy to the Memory of an Unfortunate Lady* are usually associated as the two principal examples of the impulse toward romanticism in Pope's poetry. The fact that they are both monologues, that they treat women in a somewhat similar vein, and that both concern regret for a great loss, has served to emphasize the association. The similarity, however, should not be taken for granted. Others of Pope's poems have elements of the romantic; and in detailed technique *Eloisa* and the *Unfortunate Lady* show significant differences as well as resemblances.

The *Unfortunate Lady*, for example, is not so packed with that elaborate rhetoric—the rhetorical repetition with the full range of types; the extensive exclamation and apostrophe; the rhetorical use of alliteration and even of caesura—which is the most remarkable characteristic of *Eloisa*. Yet the *Unfortunate Lady* uses interrogation quite as much and quite as well as *Eloisa*, and one of the best known examples of anaphora in all Pope is in the shorter poem:

> By foreign hands thy dying eyes were clos'd,
> By foreign hands thy decent limbs compos'd,
> By foreign hands thy humble grave adorn'd,
> By strangers honour'd, and by strangers mourn'd! (51-54)

And the *Unfortunate Lady*'s more restrained rhetoric, while never reaching the emotional felicity of certain passages in *Eloisa*, never

---

15. Ll. 99-104. Partially quoted on p. 11, above.

becomes, as *Eloisa*'s rhetoric sometimes does, monotonous, unbelievable, and self-defeating. The *Unfortunate Lady* lacks the scenic descriptions, the gloomy prospects anticipatory of the Graveyard school, for which *Eloisa* is noted; and it therefore lacks that complex pattern of repetition of sound which Pope seems to have reserved almost altogether for such descriptions. Moreover, while the *Unfortunate Lady* displays more alliteration and assonance of every kind than the *Messiah* does, yet it is nearer to that poem than to *Eloisa* in frequency of such devices.

But when Pope does use alliteration and assonance in the *Unfortunate Lady*, they bring *Eloisa* vividly to mind:

There shall the morn her earliest tears bestow,
There the first roses of the year shall blow;
While *A*ngels with their silver wings o'ershade
The ground, now sacred by thy reliques made,
(*Unfortunate Lady*, 65-68)
If ever chance two wandring lovers brings
To *P*araclete's white walls, and silver springs,
O'er the pale marble shall they join their heads,
And drink the falling tears each other sheds, (*Eloisa*, 347-350)
Cold is that breast which warm'd the world before,
(*Unfortunate Lady*, 33)
When, warm in youth, I bade the world farewell?
As with cold lips I kiss'd the sacred veil. (*Eloisa*, 110-111)

The *Unfortunate Lady* is too short for the wide variety of caesural emphasis and use of the caesura for representation which are among the finest qualities in *Eloisa*; but caesural placement in the two poems is similar, varying mainly in the greater proportion of fifth-place caesuras in *Eloisa* and of sixth-place caesuras in the *Unfortunate Lady*. And the *Unfortunate Lady* does make excellent use of the caesura for representative and rhetorical purposes:

Thence to their Images on earth/it flows, (15)
What/tho' no friends in sable weeds/appear,
Grieve for an hour,/perhaps,/then mourn a year,
And bear about/the mockery of woe
To midnight dances,/and the publick show? (55-58)

The initial trochee had by this time reached, in Pope's poetry, and was to maintain almost without exception, a frequency of about one line in four or five; but *Eloisa* is below this average, as it is in general unusually conservative (i.e., regular) in meter. The two

47

poems are similar in their variation of line and couplet structure; but in the use of the polysyllable *Eloisa* much exceeds the *Unfortunate Lady* or indeed any of the poems up to 1717 except *An Essay on Criticism.* Both poems use monosyllables more frequently than any other of the earlier poems; and both (but especially *Eloisa*) use monosyllabic lines much more frequently.

The prosodic critic feels impelled to find causes for these patterns. Since for example these are the only poems up to 1717 which are intended as *speech*—except for the very early *Pastorals,* where the speech is naturally more formal—it is not surprising that the rate of monosyllables is high; and of the poems included in this study, the three in the latter part of Pope's career which have the highest monosyllable rate—a rate almost exactly like that of *Eloisa* and the *Unfortunate Lady*—are the three which are most conversational: *Epistle to Dr. Arbuthnot,* the *First Satire of the Second Book of Horace,* and the *Epilogue to the Satires.* On the other hand, Eloisa is a learned lady, and it is not surprising that her speech should contain about as many polysyllables proportionately as *An Essay on Criticism,* the most intellectual of the early poems.

What, then, of the technical differences between *Eloisa* and the *Unfortunate Lady?* The difference between the speakers in the two poems is at least partly the difference between a man and a woman.[16] Eloisa's emotion is more profound—or less reserved—and Pope seems to have felt that greater emotion required greater regularity of form. If we nowadays are likely to stress breaks in the flow as characteristic of emotional outbursts,[17] Pope's attitude is nonetheless psychologically valid: emotion highly wrought is more rhythmical than the casual conversation of every day. And the neoclassic aesthetic would take the view that high emotion

16. "This [the difference in attitude of Priam and Hecuba] puts me in mind of a judicious stroke in Milton, with regard to the several characters of Adam and Eve. When the Angel is driving them both out of paradise, Adam grieves that he must leave a place where he had conversed with God and his angels; but Eve laments that we shall never more behold the flowers of Eden. Here Adam mourns like a man, and Eve like a woman."—Pope, note to *Iliad,* XXII, 114 (from *The Iliad of Homer,* VI, [London, 1760]). See also Tw., II, 283.
17. Lord Kames differentiates between immediate passions, such as surprise and terror, which require a broken style, and passive passions, such as melancholy, which require slow and regular movement; and he quotes from *Eloisa to Abelard,* to exemplify the latter both in passion and verse movement (pp. 238 ff.).

48

(as in Pope's model for *Eloisa*, Ovid's *Heroides*) is a heroic subject, requiring the heroic, which usually meant regular, style.[18]

Eloisa was a learned lady, and one can tell from the poem that she was a learned lady, but her learning (naturally highly rhetorical) is all subordinated to and employed for the things of the heart. All the parallels, all the antitheses, are to analyze her love and tear it to pieces. There is no logic; every time logic presents itself it is washed away in a deeper tide of feeling. The very Abelard to whom Eloisa addresses herself quite obviously feels and thinks (and not only because of his mutilation) in a way different from hers. If it is not entirely true, it is at least conventionally accepted to the point of triteness, that love is the life of a woman but only part of the life of a man. And one can easily imagine that the speaker in the *Unfortunate Lady* will do other things than mourn. He finds it possible to philosophize about his loss and to generalize this death into death as the fate of all, which makes mourning essentially futile.

His belief that the mills of the gods grind slow:

Thus, if eternal justice rules the ball,
Thus shall your wives, and thus your children fall, (35-36)

and his ability to philosophize even about this anticipated vengeance:

Thus unlamented pass the proud away,
The gaze of fools, and pageant of a day! (43-44)

are utterly different from the terrible immediacy of Eloisa's

Where, where was Eloise? her voice, her hand,
Her ponyard, had oppos'd the dire command. (101-102)

There is about Eloisa's emotion a hysteria, the hysteria of the hopelessly entrapped, an in-looking, a subordination even of the object of her love to her own feelings (she almost blames him for not suffering as she does, she wants him to pretend a physical emotion he cannot feel) which is entirely unlike the Lady's lover's essentially masculine sort of tenderness for the small and delicate and cherished (e.g., ll. 61-64), and his quite manifest ability to rise

18. On the other hand, the greater number of 5th-place caesuras in *Eloisa to Abelard* and of 6th-place in *Unfortunate Lady* may indicate greater *control* on the part of the man. Sixth-place caesuras have a quality of finality, 5th-place of tentativeness.

above his grief and return to "Life's idle business" on the way to his own grave.

The metrical regularity[19] of *Eloisa to Abelard* has, as I have said, both a psychological and an aesthetic basis; but the rules of the prosodic letter of half a dozen years before (for example, those against monosyllabic lines and non-central caesuras) were by this time being neglected far more often than in the *Pastorals*. *Eloisa* uses monosyllabic lines for as wide a variety of effects as does any poem in the canon;[20] and these lines, as well as the generally high monosyllable count, give a saving simplicity to a poem otherwise approaching the overelaborate and overwrought.

This tendency toward overelaboration is most prominent in two principal features of *Eloisa*: its pervasive and intricate rhetoric, and its equally complex and almost equally continuous employment of the devices of sound. The question, the exclamation, the apostrophe are everywhere; and while they contribute to tonal consistency, the apostrophe and exclamation particularly try to do more than they alone can. In a couplet like

O death all-eloquent! you only prove
What dust we doat on, when 'tis man we love, (335-336)

they must certainly be approved. But little can be said for such lines—and they are numerous—as

O grace serene! oh virtue heav'nly fair! (297)

Apostrophe and exclamation must seem inevitable. To use exclamation (or the exclamation point) where the emotion fails to justify it, is to risk the loss of suspension of disbelief and to approach the dubious emotionality of melodrama.[21]

It is difficult to imagine how any poem could be more crowded with rhetorical repetition and antithesis than is *Eloisa*; hardly a

19. As always, there are individual exceptions, and highly irregular lines (for Pope) do occur in *Eloisa to Abelard*, e.g., the examples on p. 10, above.
20. E.g., ll. 50, 74, 116, 118, 201, 233, 235, 289, 328, 336, 363, and two monosyllabic couplets, 123-124 and 291-292.
21. "I am inclined to think he was not much mistaken, who said, that when, on looking into a book, he found the pages thick bespangled with the point which is called 'punctum admirationis,' he judged this to be a sufficient reason for his laying it aside . . . it has now become a fashion [with "rapturous" writers] . . . to subjoin points of admiration to sentences, which contain nothing but simple affirmations, or propositions; as if, by an affected method of pointing, they could transform them in the reader's mind into high Figures of eloquence." —Blair, I, 415.

line in the poem, hardly a word, exists apart from such arrangement. Every device at the poet's command is turned to its purposes. Caesura is used:

I ought to grieve, but cannot what I ought;	4
I mourn the lover, not lament the fault;	5
I view my crime, but kindle at the view,	4
Repent old pleasures, and sollicit new. (183-186)	5

Alliteration (employed more often, probably, than in any other poem to unite substantive and adjective) reinforces all sorts of repetition in all sorts of ways:

*P*ant on thy lip, and to thy heart be *p*rest, (123)
In these deep *s*olitudes and awful *c*ells, (1)
Why *r*ove my thoughts beyond this *l*ast *r*etreat?
Why *f*eels my *h*eart its *l*ong-*f*orgotten *h*eat? (5-6)

Assonance is frequently used in the same ways:

Come b*a*nish'd lover, or some c*a*ptive maid, (52)
No cr*a*ving Void left *a*king in the breast, (94)

and alliteration and assonance together:

Her *h*eart still dict*a*tes, and her *h*and ob*ey*s. (16)

Zeugma, chiasmus, and anaphora are typical; but simple balance is more frequent, more typical. Eloisa's mind simply works—or is made to work—in pairs and in series. Almost everything is in conjunction with something else:

No pulse that riots, and no blood that glows, (252)
Excuse the blush, and pour out all the heart. (56)

Or if not that, then one thing needs repeating in a new way,[22] amplifying, developing to a climax, often and characteristically without the conjunction:

Then share thy pain, allow that sad relief, (49)
I can no more; by shame, by rage supprest, (105)
I wake—no more I hear, no more I view. (235)

And such habits of speech often continue in the most complex patterns through long series of open couplets.

Antithesis, too, is exceptionally frequent; but that Eloisa's mind, manifestly rhetorical, should have a special antithetical bent is not surprising: it represents the essence of her despair:

22. "Passion has often the effect of redoubling words."—Kames, p. 238.

51

Nor wish'd an Angel whom I lov'd a Man, (70)
I ought to grieve, but cannot what I ought, (183)
Teach me at once, and learn of me to die. (328)

Her mind seems also to work by means of true rhetorical inversion:[23]

Yet, yet I love!—From Abelard it came, (7)
No happier task these faded eyes pursue, (47)
From lips like those what precept fail'd to move? (67)
Still on that breast enamour'd let me lie. (121)

At its best all this rhetoric is so caught up into the texture of the emotion as to achieve real fusion and genuine poignancy:

No, fly me, fly me! far as Pole from Pole;
Rise Alps between us! and whole oceans roll! (289-290)
I call aloud; it hears not what I say;
I stretch my empty arms; it glides away. (237-238)

The devices of sound employed in much of this rhetoric are also used for representative purposes, especially in the elaborate patterning typical of the set descriptive passages of *Eloisa*. Indeed alliteration and assonance appear anywhere and everywhere, sometimes with unpleasant obtrusiveness:

Here grief forgets to groan, and love to weep, (314)
Thro' dreary wastes, and weep each other's woe. (242)

But even in single lines, sound repetition can have all sorts of representative purposes, as to reinforce solemnity:

Lost in a convent's solitary gloom! (38)

or to indicate apprehensive nervousness:

That well-known name awakens all my woes; (30)

or the pride of truth:

Guiltless I gaz'd; heav'n listen'd while you sung; (65)

or disdain:

What dust we doat on, when 'tis man we love; (336)

or explosive horror:

A naked Lover bound and bleeding lies; (100)

23. As in all Pope, some inversion in *Eloisa to Abelard* seems merely for the exigencies of rime; but much of it, as here, seems especially characteristic of *Eloisa* and genuinely for emphasis.

or simple determination:

> Dear fatal name! *r*est ever un*r*eveal'd,
> Nor pass these lips in holy *s*ilence *s*eal'd. (9-10).

And Pope of course uses representative meter for all the simpler types of sound and motion, of crescendo and diminuendo, which he had by this time learned thoroughly well.

More complex patterning occurs, even in passages other than pure description:

> Tho' cold l*i*ke y*ou*, unmov'd, and *si*lent grown,
>
> $\bar{o}$ $\bar{o}$ $\bar{i}$ oo oo $\bar{i}$ $\bar{o}$
>
> *I* have not yet forgot my self to stone.
>
> $\bar{i}$ $\breve{o}$ $\breve{e}$ $\bar{o}$ $\breve{o}$ $\bar{i}$ $\breve{e}$ oo $\bar{o}$ (23-24)

But the most elaborate sound repetition and representative meter in general do occur in the descriptive passages:

> The da*rks*om p*ines* that o'er yon' *rocks reclin*'d
>
> $\breve{o}$ ks $\bar{i}$n $\breve{o}$ R $\breve{o}$ ks R k $\bar{i}$n
>
> *W*ave *h*igh, and murmur to the *h*ollow *wind*,
>
> W H $\bar{i}$ H $\breve{o}$ W $\bar{i}$nd
>
> The *wand*ring str*ea*ms that sh*ine* betw*ee*n the *h*ills,
>
> W $\breve{o}$ nd $\bar{e}$ $\bar{i}$n $\bar{e}$ H
>
> The *g*ro*t*s tha*t* ec*ch*o *t*o the *t*in*k*l*i*ng *r*ills,
>
> G $\breve{o}$ t t k t t $\breve{i}$ k $\breve{i}$ $\breve{i}$
>
> The dying *g*ales tha*t p*an*t u*p*on the *t*rees,
>
> G $\bar{a}$ t p t p t
>
> The l*a*kes that *q*uive*r* to the *cur*ling breeze;
>
> $\bar{a}$ K er K er
>
> No *m*ore these scenes *m*y *m*edita*t*ion a*i*d,
>
> M M M $\bar{a}$ $\bar{a}$
>
> Or lull to rest the visionary *m*aid:
>
> M
>
> But *o*'er the tw*i*l*i*ght *g*roves, and dus*k*y *c*aves,
>
> $\bar{o}$ $\bar{i}$ l $\bar{i}$ GR $\bar{o}$ vz k k vz

53

Long-soun*ding isles*, and *intermingl*ed *graves*,

l ng n ĭ ng ī l ĭ n m ĭ ng g l GR vz

B*lack M*e*lancholy sits*, and round her throws

l k m l n k l s s

A *death-li*ke *silence*, and a *dread* re*pose*:

D ĕ l ī s ī l s D ĕ d p

Her gloomy *presence saddens* all the *scene*,

p ĕ s n s s d n s n

Shades ev'ry *flow'r*, and da*rk*ens ev'ry *gree*n,

r F r r r r ē

D*eepe*ns the m*urmur* of the *falling floods*,

ē er er F l F l

And *breathe*s a *browner* ho*rror* on the woods.

BR ē BR er r er   (155-170)

I have attempted to list all the important repetitions—surely an
amazing number—and to capitalize the alliteration. But this attempt does not begin to tell the story. Here all the stops are
opened, all techniques used: constant back vowels and liquids; all
sorts of caesural effects; long *e*'s, nasals, and voiced continuants for
smoothness; *d*'s and *s*'s in the "death-like silence" couplet; the
sudden shift to short front vowels in "tinkling rills"; onomatopoetic
words, as *lull, murmur, tinkling*; and such strictly metrical effects
as the enjambment of the first line and the weak foot (the first in
a good many lines) which precedes "falling floods"; besides the
elaborate patterning which I have pointed out. Here Pope carries
a kind of technique as far as he was ever to take it, perhaps very
nearly as far as it can go. If we today find the technique too lux-
uriant for our taste, and the material on which it is spent too dated,
such reactions should not obscure the real brilliance of this and
other similar passages in *Eloisa to Abelard*.

But if such technique and such material *are* out of date, and if
the complexity of and insistence upon rhetorical devices become
obvious and finally (to some readers at least) monotonous and
incredible in *Eloisa*, there are saving graces of technique which
make the poem not a dead relic but still a memorable poetic ex-
perience:

54

1. As a dramatic monologue, it shows deep insight. The tone, if *in*sistent, is also *con*sistent. The rhetoric, if it does at times seem superimposed, is natural to the character, and has certain individualized turns; and the voice is always the voice of a woman.

2. The rhetoric and the sound repetition occasionally reach notable heights of felicity; the emotion becomes truly pathetic and impassioned.

3. The language has at times a directness and simplicity worthy of high praise:

I have not yet forgot my self to stone, (24)
And if I lose thy love, I lose my all. (118)

4. Certain other techniques are masterly: the flow of the verse, the variations in speed, the use of enjambment and of open couplet series, and especially the variation in emphasis of pause and the use of pause for representation:

This sure is bliss/ (if bliss on earth there be), (97)
Nature stands check'd;/Religion disapproves, (259)
Spreads his light wings,/and in a moment flies, (76)
The shrines all trembled,/and the lamps grew pale. (112)

And whatever the reasons, the fact remains that *Eloisa to Abelard* can still be read with pleasure, and with no sense that the emotion is ridiculous or incongruous. One may be glad today (as intervening ages would not have been) that Pope did not continue to exploit this vein; one may find (being less accustomed to rhetorical devices than Pope's contemporaries) that the devices sometimes fail in their purposes, calling attention to themselves rather than clarifying and heightening the sense. But the requirements of verse analysis may cause an overstressing of blemishes; and one cannot deny to *Eloisa to Abelard* the four elements that make a poem of its kind successful: unity, insight, technical skill, genuine emotion. They may not all be at their highest or most consistent; but they are there.

IV

In *The Rape of the Lock,* the techniques which were turned a little later to high seriousness of purpose in *Eloisa to Abelard* are employed to nearly as great an extent for the purposes of ridicule and satire. No other branch of poetry is quite so dependent upon brilliance of style as the mock-heroic. Should it become, even for an instant, heavy-handed; should it even for a line or two lose the tone that is the mock-heroic's chief *raison d'être;* or conversely, should the continuation of the special tone become monotonous, or approach that combination of the self-conscious and the over-done which is affectation—then all would truly be lost.[24] If *The Rape of the Lock* had the technical blemishes of *Eloisa*—no more than that—it would rank far below *Eloisa* among Pope's poems.

But *The Rape of the Lock* is practically flawless. The tone is varied, and varied amply, but never fails. It is never self-conscious, never overemphasized. Using the same rhetorical methods that crowd *Eloisa*, and to a lesser extent most of the other serious poems up to 1717; exhibiting a prosodic technique rather closely related to *Eloisa*'s; using alliteration and assonance and representa-tive meter quite as much as *Eloisa*, if without *Eloisa*'s elaborate patterning—*The Rape of the Lock* would make all these methods seem as though expressly invented for the purposes of the mock-heroic, were it not that they seem also so delightfully to parody Pope's serious style.

As in *Eloisa*, the principal characteristics of *The Rape of the Lock* are its rhetoric, its use of repetition of sound, its representa-tive meter. Some of the rhetoric results, of course—as would not be true in *Eloisa*—from the requirements of epic imitation. Ex-amples are the apostrophes and questions at the beginning:

> Say what strange Motive, Goddess! cou'd compel
> A well-bred Lord t'assault a gentle Belle?
> Oh say what stranger Cause, yet unexplor'd,
> Cou'd make a gentle Belle reject a Lord? (I, 7-10)

the type of apostrophe typical of Milton:

> Ye Sylphs and Sylphids, to your Chief give Ear,
> Fays, Fairies, Genii, Elves, and Daemons hear! (II, 73-74)

the typically Homeric statements following quoted speech:

> He spoke; the Spirits from the Sails descend, (II, 137)
> She said: the pitying Audience melt in Tears; (V, 1)

and the epic similes which Pope, with a superb touch, keeps con-

---

24. *The Dunciad* is only in part a mock-heroic, stylistically, and is hence not comparable to *The Rape of the Lock*. But it suffers from the lack of unity. See Ian Jack, *Augustan Satire: Intention and Idiom in English Poetry, 1660-1750* (Oxford, The Clarendon Press, 1952, pp. 126-134).

sistently epic within themselves, allowing the mockery to appear only in the contrast with what precedes the simile and in a certain subtle overfluency of meter and phrase:

> Thus when dispers'd a routed Army runs,
> Of Asia's Troops, and Africk's Sable Sons,
> With like Confusion different Nations fly,
> Of various Habit and of various Dye,
> The pierc'd Battalions dis-united fall,
> In Heaps on Heaps; one Fate o'erwhelms them all. (III, 81-86)

In the question and the exclamation, both quite frequent in *The Rape of the Lock,* the resemblance to *Eloisa* is likely to be rather close:

> Barbarian stay! that bloody stroke restrain, (*Eloisa,* 103)
> Ah cease rash Youth! desist ere 'tis too late,
> (Rape of the Lock, III, 121)
> Oh happy state! when souls each other draw,
> When love is liberty, and nature, law, (*Eloisa,* 91-92)
> Oh thoughtless Mortals! ever blind to Fate,
> Too soon dejected, and too soon elate!
> (Rape of the Lock, III, 101-102)
> But why should I on others' pray'rs depend?
> Come thou, my father, brother, husband, friend! (*Eloisa,* 151-152)
> What tho' no Credit doubting Wits may give?
> The Fair and Innocent shall still believe.
> (Rape of the Lock, I, 39-40)

But *The Rape of the Lock,* like *Eloisa,* has turns giving it a positive individuality, distinct from the general mockery of general serious method. The exclamation is placed more variously than in *Eloisa,* and is more likely to interrupt the flow of a sentence (and hence affect the quality of the pauses):

> Not youthful Kings in Battel seiz'd alive,
> Not scornful Virgins who their Charms survive,
> Not ardent Lovers robb'd of all their Bliss,
> Not ancient Ladies when refus'd a Kiss,
> Not Tyrants fierce that unrepenting die,
> Not Cynthia when her Manteau's pinn'd awry,
> E'er felt such Rage, Resentment and Despair,
> As Thou, sad Virgin! for thy ravish'd Hair, (IV, 3-10)
> This erring Mortals Levity may call,
> Oh blind to Truth! the Sylphs contrive it all, (I, 103-104)

Spadillio first, unconquerable Lord!
Led off two captive Trumps, and swept the Board. (III, 49-50)

And the use of the exclamation point after statements, which may at times seem like straining the issue in *Eloisa*, has a natural place in lines of purposeful bathos:

Let Wreaths of Triumph now my Temples twine,
(The Victor cry'd) the glorious Prize is mine! (III, 161-162)
And all your Honour in a Whisper lost! (IV, 110)

The questions—often "rhetorical" in the special sense—are likely to be longer and more elaborate than *Eloisa*'s:

What guards the Purity of melting Maids,
In Courtly Balls, and Midnight Masquerades,
Safe from the treach'rous Friend, the daring Spark,
The Glance by Day, the Whisper in the Dark;
When kind Occasion prompts their warm Desires,
When Musick softens, and when Dancing fires? (I, 71-76)
What boots the Regal Circle on his Head,
His Giant Limbs in State unwieldy spread?
That long behind he trails his pompous Robe,
And of all Monarchs only grasps the Globe? (III, 71-74)

Two varieties of rhetoric are typical of *The Rape of the Lock* but not of *Eloisa* or indeed any other poem up to 1717: parenthesis and (naturally) anticlimax. Like the exclamation, they tend to affect the quality of the pauses; and they may also cause sudden alterations of tone which add to their significance as an element of prosody:

The Knave of Diamonds tries his wily Arts,
And wins (oh shameful Chance!) the Queen of Hearts,
(III, 87-88)
O wretched Maid! she spread her Hands, and cry'd,
(While Hampton's Ecchos, wretched Maid! reply'd), (IV, 95-96)
And sleepless Lovers,/just at Twelve,/awake, (I, 16)
Sooner let Earth, Air, Sea, to Chaos fall,
Men, Monkies, Lap-dogs, Parrots, perish all! (IV, 119-120)[25]

Only the most unlimited space could make possible a thorough-going analysis of rhetorical repetition in *The Rape of the Lock*. It

25. The emphasis, or the pitch, or both, naturally increase in this anticlimax; compare the climax of "her voice, her hand,/Her ponyard" (*Eloisa*, 101-102), in which the same intensification occurs, but without the incongruity.

is at least as frequent and of as many types as in *Eloisa*, occurs interlaced through as many series of open couplets, and displays perhaps a finer skill in variation:

> What Time wou'd spare, from *Steel* receives its date,
> And Monuments, like Men, submit to Fate!
> *Steel* cou'd the Labour of the Gods destroy,
> And strike to Dust th'Imperial Tow'rs of Troy;
> *Steel* cou'd the Works of mortal Pride confound,
> And hew Triumphal Arches to the Ground.
> What Wonder then, fair Nymph! thy Hairs shou'd feel
> The conqu'ring Force of unresisted *Steel*? (III, 171-178)

Often too it has a purposeful obviousness which is probably its most characteristic use:

> Might hide her Faults, if Belles had Faults to hide, (II, 16)
> Let Spades be Trumps! she said, and Trumps they were. (III, 46)

And Pope makes use—which has become famous—of the more special kind of zeugma, the kind which can appear only humorously or in error—and again, as so often in *The Rape of the Lock*, one result is unusual caesura:

> With earnest Eyes, and round unthinking Face,
> He first the Snuff-box open'd,/then the Case. (IV, 125-126)

Antithesis, as in *Eloisa*, is frequent (e.g., I, 54; II, 12; III, 148; V, 28), and so is the rhetorical use of alliteration and assonance. But alliteration has a special use in *The Rape of the Lock* (as occasionally does assonance) which is also rhetorical: that of making lines purposely overfacile. The device is used very often:

> The hungry Judges soon the Sentence sign, (III, 21)
> Let Wreaths of Triumph now my Temples twine, (III, 161)
> Belinda burns with more than mortal Ire,
> And fierce Thalestris fans the rising Fire, (IV, 93-94)
> And in its Fellow's Fate foresees its own. (IV, 172).

Perhaps the greatest single glory of *The Rape of the Lock*, aside from its near-perfection of tone, is its representative meter. No poem in the Pope canon, except perhaps *The Dunciad*, can equal the performance. The mastery is superb; the imitation is obvious where Pope wants it to be obvious, subtle where he prefers subtlety. It is malicious, it is devastating, it performs the most amazing tricks, it uses every technique, it never goes too far. Its principal use is to indicate littleness:

> The *light* M*i*l*i*t*i*a of the *l*ower Sky, (I, 42)
> Thin gl*i*tt'r*i*ng *T*extures of the f*i*lmy *D*ew;
> *D*ip*t* in the r*i*ches*t T*inc*t*ure of the Skies,
> Where Ligh*t d*ispor*t*s *i*n ever-m*i*ngl*i*ng *D*ies. (II, 64-66)

And there is a lightness and swiftness of both consonant and vowel characteristic of the poem as a whole which make doubly effective the contrast of the falsely big passages:

> He springs to Vengeance with an eager pace,
> And falls like Thunder on the prostrate Ace.
> The Nymph exulting fills with Shouts the Sky,
> The Walls, the Woods, and long Canals reply. (III, 97-100)

In plain contrast too is the section on the Cave of Spleen, whose difference in quality of sound and movement is well represented by its opening lines:

> Umbriel, a dusky melancholy Spright,
> As ever sully'd the fair face of Light,
> Down to the Central Earth, his proper Scene,
> Repair'd to search the gloomy Cave of Spleen. (IV, 13-16)

The light, the heavy, and still other types of sound and of movement such as rising and falling are brilliantly displayed in the passage describing the four types of supernatural creatures:

> The Sprights of fiery Termagants in Flame
> Mount up,/and take a Salamander's Name.
> *Soft* yielding M*i*nds to *W*ater gl*i*de away,
> And *si*p w*i*th N*y*m*phs*, their Elemental Tea.
> The graver Prude sinks downward to a Gnome,
> In search of Mischief still on Earth to roam.
> The *light* Coque*tt*es in S*y*l*phs* a*l*oft re*p*air,
> And *sp*ort and *fl*u*tt*er in the *F*ields of Air. (I, 59-66)²⁶

And the heavy and light also appear in the single anticlimactic line,

> Of twelve vast French Romances, neatly gilt. (II, 38)

Like everything else in *The Rape of the Lock*, the representative meter may be purposely overdone, as the *s*'s like powder escaping in

> To save the Powder from too rude a Gale,
> Nor let th'imprison'd Essences exhale; (II, 93-94)

---

26. Note also the trochaic dissyllables (*yielding, water, graver, downward, mischief*) in the second and third couplets, and the iambic dissyllables (*Coquettes, aloft, repair*) in the fourth.

the representation of sighing in

And breathes three am'rous Sighs to raise the Fire; (II, 42)

the strictness of the first line, very like files of pins, and the repeated *p*'s, indicating insignificance, of the second line, in

Here Files of Pins extend their shining Rows,
Puffs, Powders, Patches, Bibles, Billet-doux; (I, 137-138)

and the expiring quality of sound and the oversweetness in

Thus on Meander's flow'ry Margin lies
Th'expiring Swan, and as he sings he dies. (V, 65-66)

Rhetoric is turned to the uses of representation in the grotesque overstiffness of the balance in

Here living Teapots stand, one Arm held out,
One bent; the Handle this, and that the Spout. (IV, 49-50)

Among the endless imitations of movement, there is a remarkable use of meter to represent the stalking of ghosts in

And the PALE-GHOSTS-START at the FLASH-of-DAY! (V, 52)

which is one of the few lines in Pope almost completely to lose the sense of the iambic. In the whole poem, however, the greatest *tour de force* of representation, employing caesura, meter, sound repetition, sound type, and enjambment, and illustrating almost every one of the passage's complex and fantastic ideas, is the threatened punishments of irresponsible slyphs (II, 123-136).

Earlier in this study I described a type of representative meter which seems special to Pope: that of taking an important word (or words) in a couplet, analyzing the sounds, and repeating them elsewhere in the lines, often in company with obvious alliteration. Since the method is characteristically turned to the purpose of satire, it is not surprising to find Pope employing it frequently in *The Rape of the Lock* and in no other poem so far considered:[27]

(teach, flutter: *t, ē, ch* (*sh, f, l, ŭ, r*; and alliteration of *b*)
Teach Infant-*Chee*ks a *b*idden *B*lush to know,
And *li*ttle Hear*t*s to *flutter* at a *B*eau; (I, 89-90)

(Affectation: *k, t, ā, sh* (*ch*), *n*)
There Affe*cta*tion with a si*ck*ly Mien
*Sh*ows in her *Ch*eek the Roses of *Eigh*teen; (IV, 31-32)

27. It does occur notably in *An Essay on Criticism.*

61

(lisp: *l, ĭ, s* (*sh*), *p*; and alliteration of *h*)
Practis'd to *Lisp*, and *h*ang the *H*ead a*s*ide,
Faint*s* into Air*s*, and *l*angui*sh*es wit*h* Pride. (IV, 33-34)

And while the polysyllable is not so frequent in *The Rape of the Lock* as in *Eloisa to Abelard*,[28] it shows its characteristic use as an element of satire:

Spadillio first, unconquerable Lord! (III, 49)
The pungent Grains of titillating Dust. (V, 84)

With relation to the prosody, the most distinctive and noteworthy qualities of *The Rape of the Lock* seem, then, to be:

1. The great variety of effects within its sustained brilliance of tone;
2. Its general and specific resemblance in both metrics and rhetoric to *Eloisa*, the techniques of which it would seem often (if it were not the earlier poem) to parody;
3. Its purposeful use of the overfacile, in rhythm, rhetoric, repetition of sound, and representative meter;
4. The effects of epic conventions on prosody;
5. Use of all sorts of rhetoric, especially, as distinct from the other poems before 1717, zeugma in the narrow sense; exclamation as an interruption; parenthesis; and anticlimax;
6. Its unusually frequent use of enjambment;
7. The rhythm peculiar to certain of its couplets:

The pierc'd Battalions dis-united fall,
In Heaps on Heaps; one Fate o'erwhelms them all, (III, 85-86)
With store of Pray'rs, for Mornings, Nights, and Noons,
Her Hand is fill'd; her Bosom with Lampoons; (IV, 29-30)

8. The general lightness of its sounds and consequent light, swift movement; and the contrasting slowness, heaviness, and sonority of certain passages; and
9. The great variety of representative meter, employing very many techniques of meter, rhetoric, and sound; and the use of a specialized type of representative meter characteristic of Pope's satire.

V

I have not yet examined *An Essay on Criticism* because it will

28. *Eloisa*, polysyllables in 5 per cent of the lines, *Rape of the Lock*, 2 per cent. But *Rape of the Lock* has notably fewer monosyllables than *Eloisa*: 5.92 per line, compared to 6.32; and fewer monosyllable lines: 3 per cent compared to 8 per cent.

be more profitable to discuss it with its obvious companion of later years, *An Essay on Man,* and then to compare both with the (mostly) still later *Moral Essays.* Otherwise the list of Pope's important original poems up to and including the volume of 1717 is complete. Pope had gone far. Many would say that he had written his masterpiece, and certainly none of his poems have greater unity, or brilliance, or technical skill, or have worn better than *The Rape of the Lock.* Pope had, like most poets in the tradition, taken up the pastoral first, and then laid it aside forever. Except for isolated passages, he had done all that he was to do in the romantic vein. And he would never again seriously undertake anything so far from his normal bent as the *Messiah.*

He had mastered his style. With the conversational satires it was to gain an additional freedom (one cannot say *looseness*), and with the satirical portraits and *The Dunciad,* fresh *tours de force* of representative meter; but one does not deny stylistic mastery to the Shakespeare of *Twelfth Night* because he had not yet written *Othello,* and the blank verse of *Othello* is not a new thing, but a new development of the same thing, suitable to the different thought and emotion. The same (to be sure, on a lower level of Parnassus) may be said for the Pope of *The Rape of the Lock* as compared to the Pope of the *Epistle to Arbuthnot.* The tools were all in his pocket, the skill in his hands, before 1717. All he was ever to need was suitable stone.

3. THE ESSAYS

A n Essay on Criticism and *An Essay on Man* resemble each other
in such aspects of prosody and diction as moderation in the
use of the initial trochee, of polysyllables and of monosyllabic
lines, and infrequency of alliteration and other devices of sound.
This last, plus certain rhetorical matters, are of particular im-
portance, setting the two *Essays* off from the remainder of Pope's
major works, since the *Moral Essays* tend as much toward the late
satires as they do toward *An Essay on Man*. That the two *Essays*
should stand somewhat apart from the remainder of Pope's poetry
is, of course, not surprising; they are his two major poems of the
middle style, and the prosodic characteristics they display are the
characteristics to be expected.

But the materials of the two poems are not exactly the same and
the one poem is early in Pope's career, the other rather late; so
there are likely to be differences within the similarities. One evidence of this—others will appear later—is a device which occurs
infrequently but significantly in *An Essay on Criticism*, quite
frequently and more complexly in *An Essay on Man*: the sense dic-
tating unusual meter. One example from *An Essay on Criticism* is:

For Works may have more Wit than does 'em good. (303)

This monosyllabic line has only three heavy beats, there being three
words of greatly superior significance, and the result is, for Pope,
an unusual rhythmical pattern. Another example is:

Nature affords at least a glimm'ring Light. (21)

Here, to be sure, the metrical pattern remains normal, but the words
at least force a particularly heavy beat on *glimm'ring*. But the
effects in *An Essay on Man* are much more complex. Emphasis
may be forced onto normally insignificant words:

Man never IS, but always TO be blest, (I, 96)
How much OF other each is sure to cost;
How each FOR other oft is wholly lost. (IV, 271-272)

Or the emphasis may be additional rather than substitutive:

Has God, thou fool! work'd solely for THY good,

THY joy, THY pastime, THY attire, THY food?
Who for THY table feeds the wanton fawn,
For him as kindly spread the flow'ry lawn.
Is it for THEE the lark ascends and sings?
JOY tunes his voice, JOY elevates his wings. (III, 27-32)

Unusual variation and shades of accent resulting from unusual
thought patterns and word contrasts occur more often in *An Essay
on Man* than in any other major poem, and become a noticeable
part of the *Essay*'s individual texture.

Such guiding of meter by thought leads to concentration; and an
important characteristic of both *An Essay on Criticism* and *An Essay on Man* is the tightness of thought texture. The verb rate is
fairly high (higher in *An Essay on Criticism*)[1] and several other
methods of achieving succinctness occur prominently. The first
of these is unusually frequent use of special foreign constructions:

Some few in THAT, but Numbers err in THIS, (*E. on C.*, 5)
OR with a Rival's OR an Eunuch's spite, (*E. on C.*, 31)
In THIS 'tis God directs, in THAT 'tis Man, (*E. on M.*, III, 98)
Taught NOR to slack, NOR strain its tender strings.
(*E. on M.*, III, 290)

The use of the "this . . . that" pattern is often quite complex in *An
Essay on Man*:

Self-love and Reason to one end aspire,
Pain their aversion, Pleasure their desire;
But greedy THAT its object would devour,
THIS taste the honey, and not wound the flow'r, (II, 87-90)
In hearts of Kings, or arms of Queens who lay,
How happy! THOSE to ruin, THESE betray. (IV, 289-290)

This complexity would fit neither the comparatively informal tone
of *An Essay on Criticism*, nor (since the complexity often results
from using *this* and *that* through several lines) its generally more
closed couplet pattern. And in the same way, another foreign practice, the frequent and sometimes un-English use of participial
constructions, occurs in both poems for condensation, but more
often and more complexly in *An Essay on Man*:

One Science only will one Genius fit;
So vast is Art, so narrow Human Wit:
Not only *bounded* to peculiar Arts,

---

1. *E. on C.*, 1.35 verbs per line; *E. on M.*, 1.23.

But oft in those, *confin'd* to single Parts, (*E. on C.*, 60-63)
Aspiring to be Gods, if Angels fell,
Aspiring to be Angels, Men rebel, (*E. on M.*, I, 127-128)
Man, but for that, no action could attend,
And, but for this, were active to no end;
Fix'd like a plant on his peculiar spot,
To draw nutrition, propagate, and rot;
Or, meteor-like, flame lawless thro' the void,
Destroying others, by himself *destroy'd*. (*E. on M.*, II, 61-66)[2]

As a means of condensation, zeugma also occurs notably in both poems, but again with exceptional complexity in *An Essay on Man*:

And value Books, as Women Men, for Dress, (*E. on C.*, 306)
Some foreign Writers, some our own despise;
The Ancients only, or the Moderns prize, (*E. on C.*, 394-395)
Heav'n from all creatures hides the book of Fate,
All but the page prescrib'd, their present state;
From brutes what men, from men what spirits know,
(*E. on M.*, I, 77-79)
Nor this a good, nor that a bad we call,
Each works its end, to move or govern all:
And to their proper operation still,
Ascribe all Good; to their improper, Ill. (*E. on M.*, II, 55-58)

The use of lines to illustrate their own meaning is itself a means of condensation, and is of course one of the special characteristics of *An Essay on Criticism*. To warn against expletives in a line (346) which makes ill and obvious use of an expletive is certainly concentration. Some examples of this sort of thing, like the "wounded snake" Alexandrine or the passage on rime clichés, are famous; others are not, such as the strong, easy

And praise the Easie Vigor of a Line, (360)

and the slippery second line, with its early caesura, of the couplet

These leave the Sense,/their Learning to display,
And those/explain the Meaning quite away. (116-117)

Other means of condensation, such as apposition and absolute con-

---

2. On the other hand, the "there are who" pattern of un-English usage is confined to *An Essay on Criticism* (e.g., ll. 35 and 169). Oddly this usage seems to have been reserved by Pope exclusively for less formal writing, occurring again in the *Epistle to Arbuthnot* and the *First Satire of the Second Book of Horace*. The use of *who* for *he who* or *whoever* occurs in both *E. on C.* (e.g., l. 241) and *E. on M.* (e.g., IV, 59).

structions, also occur frequently. Even narrative is unusually condensed. In the Don Quixote episode in *An Essay on Criticism* Pope tells a by no means simple tale involving intricate literary theories, in the space of eighteen lines;[3] for the story of Virgil and his perusal of Homer he needs only nine. Condensation is clearly one of the fundamental qualities of the two *Essays*.

Balance is the other. The balance in *An Essay on Criticism* and *An Essay on Man* has been a source of disapprobation;[4] and in *An Essay on Criticism* it does at last become monotonous. But balance is intrinsic to the two *Essays* in a way and to an extent that it is not in any of Pope's other poems. In *Eloisa to Abelard*, for example, balance is constant, it is the material of which the poem is made. Sometimes it is especially felicitous; more often it is merely present, as the bricks of a house are present, to be accepted because without the brick the house would not be there at all. But the balance that is mere brick in *Eloisa* is in the *Essays*, as I shall presently show, a skyscraper's structural steel.

So far, the two *Essays* are alike; but the balance of which they are made is not quite the same balance, and it is integral for not quite the same reasons. The balance in *An Essay on Criticism* is for the most part exact, as it is in the other early poems; a balance of phrase by phrase, hemistich by hemistich, line by line. Such exactness is a reason for its eventual monotony. But it is intrinsic, as it is not in the other early poems[5] because the method of *An Essay on Criticism*, in big and in little, is comparison, and, more specifically, simile. And a tightly condensed development by simile leads almost inevitably to balance.

Pope depends more upon comparison in *An Essay on Criticism* and *An Essay on Man* than in any other of his poems. In his day

3. An additional means of condensation in this passage, as several other times in the two *Essays*, is unintroduced direct quotation, allowing the quoted words to speak for themselves (e.g., *E. on C.*, 383-384).

4. E.g., Tillotson, p. 137, where he says that in the two *Essays*, "Pope is using what amounts almost to a different kind of heroic couplet." Since this statement appears during a discussion of balance, one may assume that it concerns balance; and since elsewhere in his book (p. 160), Tillotson says that Pope "should not be judged by" the two *Essays*, "though even in these works the poetry has been underrated," one must assume that Tillotson does not like the methods of the *Essays*.

5. Except *The Rape of the Lock*, where the rhetorical "brick" of the other early poems is seen through the mirror of parody, and hence must be as it is because the other poems are as they are.

there were two perfectly good reasons for this: first, didactic poems were to be in the "middle" style, avoiding both the heroic high and the satirical low, and were hence to be dignified but not elaborately adorned; second, the comparisons considered—and surely properly considered—essential to illustrating and illuminating precepts and theories might adorn or amuse as well as instruct, might appropriately provide the *dulce* as well as confirm the *utile*. As Dr. Johnson was later to remark, it is only in the imagery that a didactic poem can offer anything new.

An Essay on Criticism starts out with a comparison of two different acts:

> 'Tis hard to say, if greater Want of Skill
> Appear *in Writing* or *in Judging* ill. (1-2)

Then the effect of these acts in compared:

> But, of the two, less dang'rous is th'Offence,
> To *tire our Patience*, than *mis-lead our Sense*. (3-4)

The frequency of the two acts in compared:

> *Some few in that,* but *Numbers err in this,*
> *Ten Censure wrong* for *one* who *Writes amiss*. (5-6)

Then comes a simile to illustrate and explain the prevalence of individualistic "judging" in a couplet with an unusual variant of balance pattern:

> 'Tis with *our Judgments* as *our Watches, none*
> *Go just alike,* yet *each believes his own*. (9-10)[6]

This simile is then further developed. An implied analogy is drawn from it, that since nearly everybody is prejudiced about watches, critics are likely to be prejudiced about what they criticize; and, further, that as pre-eminent poets are rare, so are pre-eminent critics:

> In *Poets* as *true Genius* is but *rare,*
> *True Taste* as *seldom* is the *Critick's* Share. (11-12)

Here the balance is line by line, with the elements slightly rearranged: a-b-c/b-c-a.

The simile of poet and critic is then clinched: each needs "light from Heav'n" in order to be a "true" member of his profession;

---

6. Here the inaccurate rime may have a purpose in illustrating the failure to "go alike."

and the relationship of "judging" and "writing" with which the poem began is again made explicit:

Both must alike from Heav'n derive their Light,
These born to Judge, as well as *those to Write.* (13-14)

The relationship of judging and writing is then extended still further: the writer should be the judge!

Let such *teach* others *who themselves excell,*
And *censure* freely *who have written well.* (15-16)

And this is the point to which the whole series of comparisons and similes has been leading. It is the advice for which the argument has prepared; and, as usual in the poem, this advice is in arrangement neat, smooth, regular, balanced, and likely to be suitable for fame as an aphorism. And then, rounding out the verse paragraph, a reason is given for the advice, offering a still further comparison of writers and judges:

Authors are partial *to their Wit,* 'tis true,
But are not *Criticks to their Judgment* too? (17-18)

But how very neat this is, and how condensed! The two ideas of writing and judging are juggled with the greatest dexterity, compared and recompared, compared to something extraneous, the comparisons extended and re-extended, through closed couplet after closed couplet. Words are compared, and phrases, and clauses, and lines. And yet not only is the balance an integral part of the method, not only do its neatness and aptness give it a share in the wit of the lines, but also it is made various and positively sprightly because of changes in the length and in the order of the balanced elements; because of frequent enjambment within the couplets, especially the strong run-on after the ninth line; because of the lightness of the vowels and consonants; and particularly because, in spite of the balance and the careful train of argument, the word order and the tone are often astonishingly colloquial.

It is impractical, of course, to continue such a couplet-by-couplet analysis throughout the poem. But one finds next, for instance, the mind compared to a well-drawn sketch; and the mind ill-taught to a well-drawn sketch ill-colored. This is used as the basis for explaining why those who cannot write often become critics. Those who cannot even be critics are then compared to mules, and—in a passage which is the first faint glimmering of such later satirical

69

portraits as that of Sporus—to insects:

Those *half-learn'd Witlings*, num'rous *in our Isle*,
As *half-form'd Insects on the Banks of Nile.* (40-41)

Soon after, comes an explanation of mental limitations based on the simile that all land cannot at once be dry; and then (in another shift of simile) if we attempt to overcome that inevitable limitation,

Like Kings we lose the Conquests gain'd before,
By vain Ambition still to make them more. (64-65)

The pattern is becoming, as it must, slightly looser, and the couplets more open, but the method is still the same. In one couplet the simile will be almost casual:

For Wit and Judgment often are at strife,
Tho' meant each other's Aid, *like Man and Wife.* (82-83)

In the next, the simile has become metaphor, and the comparison is inseparable from the meaning—yet the balance remains:

'Tis more to *guide than spur* the Muse's Steed;
Restrain his Fury, than provoke his Speed. (84-85)

Ancient Greece is then held up in some detail as an example of cooperation between critic and poet; and we are shown what has happened with that cooperation gone: critics nowadays are like apothecaries (108-111), moths (113), cooks (115). And again the advice:

Be Homer's Works your Study, and Delight,
Read them by Day, and meditate by Night. (124-125)

Then, presently, the comparison of poetry to music; the famous Pegasus simile; and further illuminating similes, of precipices and kings and law, of armies and altars and streams, to the end of the first part of the poem—and with balance closely involved all the way.[7]

The method continues through the remainder of the poem. There is the "Pierian spring"; the long simile of the Alps which Dr. Johnson thought probably the best in all English literature;[8] the exemplum of "La Mancha's Knight"; loquacity like leaves;

7. The balance is especially frequent with verbs: besides the "judge-write" pairs of ll. 1-18, there are prevails, fails; stoop, understand; feed, fills; guides, sustains; guide, spur; restrain, provoke; discover'd, devis'd; restrain'd, ordain'd; repress, indulge; winn, woo'd; hate, learn'd; cavil, criticise; read, meditate; offend, mend; nods, dream; glows, trembles; admire, doubt; and others.

8. *Life of Pope, Lives of the English Poets*, II, 218.

truth like the sun; false eloquence like a prism; conceits like a clown; the "wounded snake" Alexandrine; narrowness of wit like narrowness of religion; envy like the moon; unwarranted suspicion like the yellow of jaundice; Appius like a tapestry tyrant; and a good many more. Only in the third part, with its lengthy tour through the history of criticism, does the balance undeniably grow tiresome; and it is in the third part that the similes and other comparisons are fewest, and the method therefore least organic. And the third part is also least colloquial in tone.

Pope uses comparatively little ornament of sound in *An Essay on Criticism*—in strong contrast to such poems as *Windsor-Forest* and *Eloisa to Abelard*—and, except for the illustrative representation in Part II, not even much representative meter. He rarely supports the balance with alliteration; and when he does, it seems in consequence especially emphatic:

> Without all these at once before your Eyes,
> Cavil you may, but never Criticize. (122-123)

Extremely unlike *Eloisa*, he uses only the fewest alliterative adjective-substantive combinations. "Lucky Licence" (148) and "constant Critick" (416) are among the rare, almost casual instances; and one famous couplet is given particular point by the sudden, full-blown use of so very occasional a method:

> The Bookful Blockhead, ignorantly read,
> With Loads of Learned Lumber in his Head. (612-613)

It is the same with other types of alliteration. Lines like

> Correctly cold, and regularly low, (240)

are scarce enough to make one believe that Pope not only seldom sought alliteration in *An Essay on Criticism* but in general strove actively to avoid it. And of assonance there is even less.

Such representative meter as exists beyond the special illustrative kind in Part II is largely representation of motion, or is satirical; and it depends mainly upon meter, caesura, and enjambment, rather than sound patterns:

> Which,/without passing thro' the Judgment,/gains
> The Heart/, (156-157)

> Where a new World leaps out at his command, (486)

> The Memory's soft Figures melt away. (59)[9]

9. Note how completely the special "melting" quality of this line would

71

There is, of course, fine use of the polysyllable for satire:

> Fear most to tax an Honourable Fool, (588)
> And charitably let the Dull be vain. (597)

Rime, too, is used, and used well, for satire; and rime is one of Pope's characteristic excellences in *An Essay on Criticism* (e.g., ll. 354-355, 416-417).[10]

One instance does occur of elaborate patterning and more complex representative meter:

> *Mo*der*ns*, beware! Or if you *must* off*end*

> m d n m st ĕ n d

> A*gainst* the *Precept*, *ne'er* trans*gress* its *End*,

> gĕ n st p s ĕ p t n ĕ t n s g ĕ s t s ĕ n d

> *Let* it be *seldom*, and *compell'd* by *Need*,

> l ĕ t t s ĕld um um p ĕld n ē d

> And have, a*t least*, Th*eir Prece*d*ent to plead.*

> t l ē s t ĕ p ĕ s d t t p l ē d

> The Cri*tick else proceeds* without Remorse.

> t ĕ l s p s ē d s   (163-167)

Here the stiff preciseness of the *d*'s, *t*'s, and *p*'s, the short *e*'s, the obvious, clear-cut alliteration and assonance, and the regular, rapid meter work as a sharp satirical thrust against the law.

Several examples occur of representative meter of the special "sound-analysis" type. Sometimes, since there is no prominent word or words on which to pin it, it is not yet quite in complete form:

> Dis*charge* that *R*age on *more* P*ro*v*ok*ing *C*ri*mes*,
> No*r fear* a D*earth* in these *F*la*gitious* Times. (528-529)[11]

---

be lost if *Memory* were made to fill two half-feet instead of three, e.g.:
    The Memory's softest figures melt away.
Yet confining such a word to two half-feet was overwhelmingly the normal practice of Pope and his period, here abandoned for a special purpose.

10. See also p. 26, above. Good satirical rime likewise occurs in triplets (ll. 328-330), and in feminine rime (ll. 442-443). But *E. on C.* has also numerous instances of poor rime correspondence (e.g., ll. 139-140, 301-302, 588-589), and not all its feminine rimes are successful (e.g., ll. 592-593).

11. Besides the prominent *j* sounds in *discharge*, *rage*, and *flagitious*, note the closely related *ch* and *sh* sounds in the first and last of these words.

Sometimes it is in full flower:[12]

(tremendous, eye: *t, r, ē, m, ĕ, n, s, ī*)
And *stares, Tremendous!* with a threatning *Eye,*
Like some fierce Tyrant in Old *Tapestry!* (586-587)

But these examples of ornament and representation are tiny islands in oceans of speech not so elaborated; and Pope lets pass many obvious opportunities for representation, notably the description of climbing the Alps (ll. 225-232) and at least one of the embryonic satirical portraits (ll. 414-423).[13] If it seems strange that in a poem noted for extolling representative meter there should be so little of it, it should be remembered that continuous elaborate patterning and representation would be out of place in a didactic, colloquial, unimpassioned work. Balance, condensation, and comparison remained, as they almost surely should have, the primary methods.

Balance, condensation, and comparison are the methods in *An Essay on Man* too, but the balance is a different balance, and springs from a somewhat different cause. In striking contrast to the earlier *Essay*, Epistle I of *An Essay on Man* has no similes whatever. In it, and less frequently throughout the remainder of *An Essay on Man*, the method of illustration (and of ornamentation) is by examples from other links in the chain of being;[14] and, since Pope's desire is usually to point up the correspondence in some detail, the comparison is likely to be extended to greater length than in the earlier *Essay*. So, there is the lamb which illustrates a complex proposition:

Heav'n from all creatures hides the book of Fate,
All but the page prescrib'd, their present state;
From brutes what men, from men what spirits know:
Or who could suffer Being here below?
The lamb thy riot dooms to bleed to-day,
Had he thy Reason, would he skip and play?
Pleas'd to the last, he crops the flow'ry food,
And licks the hand just rais'd to shed his blood. (I, 77-84)

12. One of the finest examples from *E. on C.* has already been given on p. 33, above.
13. Two more of the embryonic portraits (ll. 36-43 and 328-332) show some evidence of satirical sound-patterning.
14. Cf. Parkin, p. 76.

Or the proposition may be clinched by a series of parallels from the chain:

> Ask of thy mother earth, why oaks are made
> Taller or stronger than the weeds they shade?
> Or ask of yonder argent fields above,
> Why Jove's Satellites are less than Jove? (I, 39-42)

This method comes to a climax in Epistle I with the famous series of comparisons of senses, including the potential "aromatic pain" from the rose, and the fine touch of the spider; and, following this, with the series of comparisons extending "from Infinite to thee, from thee to Nothing," which occur toward the end of the Epistle. Individual images in these passages rarely extend beyond a single couplet; but the comparison usually runs through at least four, and often through many more lines.

Epistle II also draws comparisons from the chain of being:

> Fix'd like a plant on his peculiar spot,
> To draw nutrition, propagate, and rot;
> Or, meteor-like, flame lawless thro' the void,
> Destroying others, by himself destroy'd. (63-66)

But the emphasis here falls on the similes—and note that they *are* similes—rather than on the parallel, and is hence more reminiscent of *An Essay on Criticism* than of the first Epistle of *An Essay on Man*. In the extended simile of the Alps in *An Essay on Criticism*, the student is not parallel to the mountain-climber; the comparison illuminates and has no further intention. In the comparison of the lamb in Epistle I of *An Essay on Man*, on the other hand, the comparison involves a parallel: man is to God as lamb is to man. But in the passage just quoted from Epistle II, while the comparison is drawn from the chain of being, no true parallel is involved: without Reason, man would not in actuality "flame lawless through the void," nor is it the lack of Reason which causes a meteor to do so. The comparison simply illuminates.

And throughout Epistle II, the method is for the most part simile (and metaphor) as in *An Essay on Criticism*: there are more than a dozen actual similes in Epistle II and a good many more metaphors. Some of them, like most in *An Essay on Criticism*, are brief:

> In Folly's cup still laughs the bubble, joy; (288)

74

In lazy Apathy let Stoics boast
Their Virtue fix'd; 'tis fix'd as in a frost. (101-102)

The idea of light and darkness, on the other hand, continues through fourteen lines (203-216); and even the "Ask where's the North?" analogy, which in tone and idea resembles the two-line comparison of watches in *An Essay on Criticism*, extends through nine (222-230).

In the last two Epistles, the methods are more equally balanced: a good many illustrations from the chain appear, but fewer than in Epistle I; some similes, but not nearly so many as in Epistle II. But the comparisons are still likely to be considerably longer than those in *An Essay on Criticism*. And as is justified by the more serious material and tone, the comparisons throughout *An Essay on Man* are more often than in the earlier *Essay* "ennobling" (as Dr. Johnson put it) in addition to being illustrative.[15]

But as the comparisons in *An Essay on Man* are different, so is the balance. As the comparisons are often more extended and less neat, so is the balance more complex, more varied, and less exactly balanced than that in *An Essay on Criticism*. (And hence, too, *An Essay on Man* has many more open couplet sequences than its predecessor.) The balancing elements may be in the last line of one couplet and the first of the next:

Breathes in our soul, informs our mortal part,
As full, as perfect, in a hair as heart;
As full, as perfect, in vile Man that mourns, (I, 275-277)
He hangs between; *in doubt* to act, or rest,
In doubt to deem himself a God, or Beast;
In doubt his Mind or Body to prefer. (II, 7-9)

Among the extremely various uses of word repetition, one kind especially characteristic of *An Essay on Man* is repetition of key words with shifts in form, context, grammar, or connotation:[16]

Re-judge his justice, be the God of God! (I, 122)
Grows with his growth, and strengthens with his strength,

(II, 136)

---

15. E.g., III, 285-295; IV, 7-16. Some images do sound very like *E. on C.*, however:
But honest Instinct comes a volunteer, (III, 88)
Who bid the stork, Columbus-like, explore. (III, 105)
16. Most of these examples fall under the technical rhetorical heading of polyptoton.

See dying vegetables life sustain,
See life dissolving vegetate again. (III, 15-16)

And especially the arrangement of balancing elements may be very complicated:[17]

   (a)   (b)   (b)   (c)
Who noble ends by *noble means obtains,*
           (c)   (d)   (d)
Or failing, *smiles in exile* or *in chains,*
     (e)   (a) (f)   (f)
Like good Aurelius let *him reign,* or *bleed*
     (e)   (a)
Like Socrates, that Man is great indeed! (IV, 233-236)

In longer passages, arrangements may become even more complex:

     (a)   (a)   (a)
See, thro' *this air, this ocean,* and *this earth,*
      (b)   (b)
All matter *quick,* and *bursting* into birth.
  (c)   (d)   (e)
Above, how high progressive life may *go*!
  (c)   (d)   (d)   (e)   (c)
Around, how wide! *how deep extend below*!
  (ABCDEF . . .)   (A)
Vast chain of being, which from *God* began,
    (B)   (C) (B) (C)
Natures aethereal, human, angel, man,
 (D) (E) (F) (G) (H) (f) (g) (h) (i)
Beast, bird, fish, insect! *what no eye can see,*
 (f) (g) (h) (i)   (j)   (A) (k) (C)
No glass can reach; *from Infinite to thee,*
 (j) (C) (k) (H)   (l)   (AB)
From thee to Nothing!—*On superior pow'rs*
   (C)   (m) (DEFGH) (m) (l) (C)
Were *we* to *press, inferior might on ours*;
    (BCDEF . . .) (m)
Or in the *full creation leave* a void,
  (B or C or . . .) (n)   (ABCDEF . . .) (n)
Where, *one step broken,* the *great scale's destroy'd*:
  (ABCDEF . . .)   (B or C or . . .)   (n)
From *Nature's chain* whatever *link* you *strike,*

17. Far more so indeed than the examples offered by Tillotson (p. 128).

(B* or C* or . . .) (B** or C** or . . .) (n) (ABCDEF . . .)
Tenth   or   ten   thousandth,   breaks   the   chain alike.
(I, 233-246)

Clearly this elaboration of arrangement of balanced elements goes far beyond anything in *An Essay on Criticism*.

Besides the methods of balance and repetition, Pope uses two other rhetorical devices especially frequently in *An Essay on Man*: exclamation and interrogation. Exclamation needs no re-examining. It is as common as in the *Messiah*, in the heightened passages of *Windsor-Forest*, in *Eloisa to Abelard*, for similar reasons and with much the same result. Interrogation is another matter. If the tone of any poem of Pope's is affected by a rhetorical device not involving balance, *An Essay on Man*'s tone is affected by its questions. In Epistle I alone there are nearly thirty, in Epistle IV nearly fifty. Many of them are scornful:

All this dread Order break—for whom? for thee? (I, 257)
Oh sons of earth! attempt ye still to rise,
By mountains pil'd on mountains, to the skies? (IV, 73-74)

Sometimes they are placed in the mouth of "man" in order to be demolished:

"Why bounded Pow'r? why private? why no king?"
Nay, why external for internal giv'n?
Why is not Man a God, and Earth a Heav'n?
Who ask and reason thus, will scarce conceive
God gives enough, while he has more to give. (IV, 160-164)

More frequently they are rhetorical in the narrow sense, directing their own implicit answer:

The lamb thy riot dooms to bleed to-day,
Had he thy Reason, would he skip and play? (I, 81-82)

Occasionally, however, they are asked in order to be answered:

Why has not Man a microscopic eye?
For this plain reason, Man is not a Fly. (I, 193-194)

The device seems overdone, though many of the individual questions are effective, and interrogation is a proper rhetorical device in a philosophical poem. The issue is whether or not, by calling attention to method and away from meaning, the abundance of questions may not contribute to a sameness of tone, and a decrease in force. Interrogation in *An Essay on Man* stands with exclama-

77

tion in *Eloisa to Abelard* among the very few instances in which Pope's judgment did not altogether preclude excess.

Pope's use of alliteration, assonance, and representative meter in *An Essay on Man* resembles that in *An Essay on Criticism* but is not quite so restricted. The long section of Epistle I concerned with the comparative keenness of the senses is almost as famous for its representation as the section of illustrative representation in the earlier *Essay*. There is the grotesqueness of

How Instinct varies in the grov'ling swine,
Compared, half-reas'ning elephant, with thine. (I, 221-222)

There is the delicate rhythm and music of

Or *touch*, if *tremblingly* alive all o'er. (I, 197)

And there is the sensitive accuracy and patterning of

The sp*ider's touch*, how exqui*sitely* fine!
Feels at each thread, and *lives* along the *line*. (I, 217-218)

Some very elaborate sound arrangements occur:

Far as Cre*ation's* a*mp*le *range extends*,

ā sh n m p ā n ĕ ĕ n

The *scale* of *sensual, mental pow'rs ascends*:

s ā s ĕ n sh m ĕ n p s ĕ n

*M*ark how it *mounts*, to *M*an's im*perial race*,

m m n m n m p ē

From the *green myriads* in the *peopled grass*:

gr ē n m ē p ē p gr

What *modes* of *sight* be*twixt each wide extreme*,

m ō d ī t t w ĭ x t ē w ī d x t ē m

The *mole's dim* curtain, and the *lynx's beam*.

m ō d ĭ m t ĭ x ē m   (I, 207-212)

Like *An Essay on Criticism, An Essay on Man* includes several instances of "word-analysis" representation; one excellent example, a reminder of the other very different poems being written at the time of *An Essay on Man*, is

(politic, sly: *p, l, t, ĭ, k, s, ī*)
No *less* a*like* the *Politic* and W*ise*,
All *sly slow* things, with *circumspective eyes*. (IV, 225-226)

78

As in *An Essay on Criticism*, Pope uses caesura,[18] enjambment, and polysyllables well, and rime, including feminine rime,[19] both well (though not nearly so often for satire) and badly, committing more bad rimes than in any other major poem. And as in *An Essay on Criticism*, he passes over numerous opportunities for representation, for example the "lamb" and "poor Indian" passages in Epistle I, and the piling on of mountains in Epistle IV.

The tone of the poem is much more formal than that of the earlier *Essay*. There is considerably more inversion; few lines are colloquial in tone; and several heightened passages are of great intensity. Accordingly, caesuras appear later in the line somewhat more frequently, and in the heightened passages much more frequently.[20] Accordingly, too, the quality of vowels and consonants is darker. The poem often flows powerfully through a long series of open couplets. And the tone is varied more widely than in *An Essay on Criticism*. The "poor Indian" passage, for instance, is quiet with a regular, light beat, while the passage ending with the following lines has an increasing loudness, heaviness of beat, and swiftness of movement that is almost dizzying:

Let ruling Angels from their spheres be hurl'd,
Being on being wreck'd, and world on world,
Heav'n's whole foundations to their centre nod,
And Nature tremble to the throne of God. (I, 253-256)

Such passages have a power equalled nowhere else in Pope except in *The Dunciad*, an emotional depth which only the close of *The Dunciad* can match.

Pope also composes in *An Essay on Man*—as occasionally in *An Essay on Criticism* but much more frequently in his later career—many neat, accurate, "right" lines which illustrate no one skill but have that quality of inevitability which marks the fine artist and is "beyond the reach of art" to analyze:

18. E.g.:
Created half to rise,/and half to fall, (II, 15)
And turn'd on Man a fiercer savage,/Man. (III, 168)
19. Including one of the best and best-known in Pope:
What can ennoble sots, or slaves, or cowards?
Alas! not all the blood of all the Howards. (IV, 215-216)
Bad feminine rimes occur at IV, 203-204, and IV, 277-278.
20. My reading of *E. on M.*, Epistle I, shows 43 per cent of the caesuras to come after the 4th syllable or earlier, whereas in six of the "heightened" passages in the poem (I, 85-90, 113-130, 247-258, 267-280, 289-294, and II, 3-18), only 26 per cent after the 4th syllable or earlier. Count after 6th syllable or later: Epistle I, 23½ per cent; "heightened" passages, 36 per cent.

> And Passions are the elements of Life, (I, 170)
> To draw nutrition, propagate, and rot, (II, 64)
> To welcome death, and calmly pass away, (II, 260)
> Entangle Justice in her net of Law, (III, 192)
> Because he wants a thousand pounds a year. (IV, 192)

These are in addition to the many aphorisms which have become a part of the language.

In summary then, *An Essay on Criticism* and *An Essay on Man* are similar in their use of condensation, balance, and comparison, in infrequency of sound patterning and representation, and in various aspects of meter. But, while both are in the middle style, the materials are quite different. And hence it is not surprising, on the basis of Pope's often-voiced creed that style must match subject matter not only from poem to poem but within a poem, that the comparisons in the two *Essays* are different comparisons and the balance a different balance; and moreover that the one poem is often colloquial in its diction, simple in its rhetoric, cool, witty, light in tone color, lacking in flow, while the other is usually dignified in its diction, often complex in its rhetoric, frequently sonorous, occasionally impassioned, with long, open verse-paragraphs of almost Miltonic flow. The purpose was didactic in both, but the materials were dissimilar; nor would Pope have been the man to forget that, while Horace is the progenitor of *An Essay on Criticism*, he is only the co-progenitor, with Lucretius, of *An Essay on Man*.[21]

II

In technique and tone, Pope's *Moral Essays*[22] represent a transition from *An Essay on Man* to the Horatian satires and epistles.

---

21. See Reuben A. Brower, *Alexander Pope: the Poetry of Allusion* (Oxford, The Clarendon Press, 1959), pp. 207, 216-217.

22. Tw. (III, ii, xxxvi-xxxvii) offers cogent reasons why the alternate title for these poems, *Epistles to Several Persons*, is better. I call them *Moral Essays* purely for reasons of convenience: to connect them with *An Essay on Man*, with which the same passage in Tw. says they are to be associated, and to differentiate them from the imitations of Horatian satires and epistles. Tw. also points out quite properly that the *Moral Essays* resemble Horatian epistles; but they do not resemble Horatian epistles as closely as the *Epistle to Arbuthnot* and the *Epilogue to the Satires* do; and even the second *Moral Essay*, which most nearly resembles *Arbuthnot*, the *Epilogue*, and the Horatian imitations, is like the other *Moral Essays* in dealing with the ruling passions (as the major Horatian poems do not), is less Horatian in its subject matter generally than

The third *Essay*, that to Bathurst, with its serious tone and many questions, resembles *An Essay on Man* most nearly. The portraits and stories, its most memorable feature, do not much resemble the portraits in the other *Moral Essays*, being long and grave with the late caesuras for heightened passages,[23] and the flow, and at least something of the complex balance and the formality of *An Essay on Man*; and even the uncomplimentary portraits do not have the concentration and the representative ugliness of many in the other *Essays* and in the Horatian satires. But the third *Moral Essay* opens as colloquially and casually as any of the satires:

Who shall decide, when Doctors disagree,
And soundest Casuists doubt, like you and me? (1-2)

Like *An Essay on Man*, it has very little representative meter; but it has the rather frequent alliteration on balanced parts which is typical of Pope in general but relatively infrequent in *An Essay on Man*:

*St*atesman and *P*atriot *p*ly alike the *st*ocks,
*P*eeress and *B*utler share alike the *B*ox,
And *J*udges *j*ob, and *B*ishops *b*ite the town. (141-143)

As in *An Essay on Man*, Pope uses very unusual anaphora:

Cutler saw tenants break, and houses fall,
For very want; he could not build a wall.
His only daughter in a stranger's power,
For very want; he could not pay a dow'r. (323-326)

But in spite of a casual power of line and phrase, the tone is quieter than *An Essay on Man's*, and the serious passages become neither overwrought on the one hand nor sublime on the other.

---

the Horatian group, and is unlike the Horatian group in certain technical aspects, having, for example, far fewer monosyllables and verbs than the four major Horatian poems, and resembling them, where it does, where they are less typical and more formal (the *Epistle to Augustus* and the *Epilogue*) rather than the reverse (*Arbuthnot* and the *First Satire of the Second Book*). Also *Moral Essays*, I and II, are almost identical in their caesural pattern. At any rate, this study demonstrates that the *Moral Essays* are transitional prosodically between *An Essay on Man* and the Horatian group. (Chronologically, the pattern is, of course, far from neat: see the chronology in Tw., and the discussion in Sherburn, *Best of Pope*, pp. 420 ff.)

23. The story of Sir Balaam has 24 per cent sixth-place caesuras. In contrast, even the heightened passage of the first *Moral Essay*, 174-209, has only 6 per cent.

Nevertheless, quieter, less formal, less complex though it is, the third *Moral Essay* is the closest to *An Essay on Man* of any poem in the group.

Next must be placed the fourth *Moral Essay*, that to Burlington. It moves toward the satires in being more personal, and hence more colloquial. It is more mocking in its satire than the third, and has indeed more satire; and—like *An Essay on Criticism* in that and in this—it has fewer fine passages than *An Essay on Man*, but a good many fine lines:

> Think we all these are for himself? no more
> Than his fine Wife, alas! or finer Whore, (11-12)
> Blushing in bright diversities of day. (84)

It has somewhat more representative meter than the third, but on the other hand not as much alliteration or assonance. It has fewer questions, little pathos or intensity, but on the other hand it has no portraits. It is closer to the satires, then, in general tone, but not much closer in detail.

The first *Moral Essay*, that to Cobham, moves considerably further toward the satires, even though in subject matter it is of the four most like *An Essay on Man*. Excepting the Sir Balaam story in the third *Essay*, the first displays a more brilliant versification than either the third or the fourth. It has a passage of considerable intensity in the lines beginning

> Search then the Ruling Passion: There, alone,
> The Wild are constant, and the Cunning known. (174-175)

But the intensity and the anger recall *An Essay on Man* less than they anticipate the *Epilogue to the Satires*, with its

> Hear her black Trumpet thro' the Land proclaim,
> That "Not to be corrupted is the Shame." (I, 159-160)

The first *Essay* has many questions, but they are calmer than *An Essay on Man*'s, more varied, and more artful:

> Is he a Churchman? then he's fond of pow'r:
> A Quaker? sly: A Presbyterian? sow'r:
> A smart Free-thinker? all things in an hour. (107-109)

It has, like the third *Essay* (and also the second), a casual beginning; and its general tone is quieter, more of discussion than lecture, with a lighter quality of sound. It is notably condensed—its stories are even more amazingly compact than those in *An Essay on Criticism*; and it combines the examples of *An Essay on Man* with comparisons reminiscent of *An Essay on Criticism*:

> Nature well known, no prodigies remain,
> Comets are regular, and Wharton plain, (208-209)

and of *An Essay on Man*:

> Tho' the same Sun with all-diffusive rays
> Blush in the Rose, and in the Diamond blaze,
> We prize the stronger effort of his pow'r,
> And justly set the Gem above the Flow'r. (97-100)

Being largely made up of brief portraits and examples of ruling passions, it has little of *An Essay on Man*'s openness of couplet series.

Alliteration, assonance, and repetition of sounds in general rise considerably above any of the poems so far examined in this chapter:

> The *coxc*omb bird, so tal*k*ative and grave,
> That from his *c*age *c*ries *Cuck*old, Whore, and Knave, (5-6)
> Perha*ps* Pros*pe*rity be*c*alm'd his *breast*, (63)
> When uni*v*ersal homage *Um*bra *p*ays,
> All see 'tis *V*ice, and itch of *v*ulgar *p*raise. (118-119)

Alliteration of adjective and substantive notably reappears; for example, varying vein (16); flat Falshood (126); perjur'd Prince (148); charming Chintz (244). There are several instances of special representation:

> (sneaks: *s, n, ē, k*)
> Will *sneaks* a Scriv'ner, an ex*cee*ding k*n*ave, (106)

> (hates, Shylock: *h, t, sh* (*ch*), *ī, l, ŏ, k*)
> And ev'ry *child hates Shylock*, tho' his *soul*
> *Still sits at squat*, and peeps *n*ot from *its hole*. (114-115)

But other representative meter is still infrequent, and there is little or no ornamental patterning. Rime is used excellently for satire; and the closing series of portraits, with the directly quoted speech of the satirized, are as colloquial as anything in Pope.

Yet, besides the questions, the examples, and the one passage of some intensity, other reminders of *An Essay on Man* still remain. Balance breaks across line and couplet:

> Who would not praise Patritio's high desert,
> His hand unstain'd, his uncorrupted heart,

83

His comprehensive head! (140-142)
Wise, if a Minister; but, if a King,
More wise. (91-92)

Unusual anaphora and polyptoton appear:

Who does a kindness, is not therefore kind . . . .
Who combats bravely is not therefore brave . . . .
Who reasons wisely is not therefore wise, (62, 67, 69)
Ask why from Britain Caesar would retreat?
Caesar himself might whisper he was beat.
Why risk the world's great empire for a Punk?
Caesar perhaps might answer he was drunk, (81-84)
And most contemptible, to shun contempt. (195)

And, as in all the *Moral Essays*, Pope creates lines of casual power:

A bird of passage! gone as soon as found, (156)
And wanting nothing but an honest heart. (193)

The second *Moral Essay* is of the four the most mockingly satirical, the most colloquial, the least of all like *An Essay on Man*,
of which almost nothing is left. The second *Moral Essay* is a sort
of *Rape of the Lock*, with malice and informality put in and
story and epic machinery left out. It is light-weight, it is alliterative,
it is quick, it has the most brilliant rimes (including feminines)
and polysyllables, the most wittily malicious representative meter.
 Some passages might have been lifted straight out of *The Rape
of the Lock*; for example, the deliberate oversweetness of

Or drest in *smiles* of *sweet Cecil*ia sh*ine*,
With *simp'ring* Angels, Palms, and Har*ps* di*vine*; (13-14)
the light vowels, delicate pauses, and breathless parentheses of

Come then, the colours and the ground prepare!
Dip in the Rainbow, trick her off in Air,
Chuse a firm Cloud, before it fall, and in it
Catch, ere she change, the Cynthia of this minute; (17-20)

the prominently placed insignificant simile and the casual alliteration of

Ladies, like variegated Tulips, show,
'Tis to their Changes half their charms we owe; (41-42)

and the bathos, resulting from the overexact meter, the alliteration,
the trisyllables, the repetition, applied to an inadequate cause, of

A Park is purchas'd, but the Fair he sees
All bath'd in tears—"Oh odious, odious Trees!" (39-40)

But other brilliances are of another kind. *The Rape of the Lock* was never so deliciously colloquial as

Whether the Charmer sinner it, or saint it,
If Folly grows romantic, I must paint it. (15-16)[24]

It had not quite the same careless-seeming yet perfect use of the polysyllable as in

Let then the Fair one beautifully cry, (11)
So these their merry, miserable Night. (240)

It had not the purposeful ugliness (as in the late satires) of

As Sappho's *di*amonds with her *dirty sm*ock,
Or *S*appho *a*t her *toilet's* greasy *ta*sk,
With *S*appho fragrant at an evening *M*ask:
So *m*orning In*s*ects that in *muck* beg*un*,
Shine, *buzz*, and fly-*blow* in the *s*etting-*sun*. (24-28)

It had not the combination of light regular meter, perfect rime, and utterly repugnant idea which makes the following couplet so memorable—and so reminiscent of Swift:

Narcissa's nature, tolerably mild,
To make a wash, would hardly stew a child. (53-54)

The longer central portraits—Flavia, Atossa, Chloe, and so on—are very like the portraits in the *Epistle to Arbuthnot*. And the close of the poem, with its praise of Martha Blount, turns, as so often in Pope, personal and quiet, though this time never quite losing a certain mockery—it might almost be called whimsy—which appears not only in the words, but also in the caesuras, the balance, the rime.

The poem is the most distinctive of the *Moral Essays*. Women, says Pope, are light-weight and given dazzlingly to change. The versification is likewise. Except perhaps in the portraits of Philomedé and Atossa, one never forgets that the poem represents conversation not only about women, but with a woman. One would be hard put to it to match it for light, knowing, scintillating, concentrated gossip.

---

24. Which is, so to speak, the feminine gender of "Fools rush into my head, and so I write" (*First Satire of the Second Book of Horace*, 14).

4. LATE AND SATIRICAL

Pope's greatest achievement in versification is very likely the combination of a concentrated brilliance of statement and of special metrical effect, with a colloquial tone. In real life, of course, no one ever spoke so well, every word in place, every word not only *mot juste* but *mot juste inattendu.* In real life, the wittiest conversationalist often only approximates what he intended to say—and the wittiest conversationalist is not always at his wittiest. The artist must make dull speech interesting, and intelligent speech brilliant, or we shall not enjoy it. He must give it that Protean quality, verisimilitude, or we shall reject it, as stiff or strained, sentimental or ranting, out of character or out of style or out of place. Iambic pentameter, rimed, does not make the task easier. Yet it is in the satires and epistles that Pope's verse form most truly justifies itself. It is just possible to conceive of *The Dunciad* in blank verse or *Eloisa to Abelard* in rime royal. But the satires display such a triumphant wedding of form to matter, such a complete bending of means to requirements, that that fact itself is no small part of the pleasure.

My examination of Pope's Horatian satires and epistles concentrates on the four major poems: *The Epistle to Arbuthnot*, the *First Satire of the Second Book of Horace*, the *Epistle to Augustus* (*First Epistle of the Second Book of Horace*), and the *Epilogue to the Satires.* The others certainly have good lines:

> The modern language of corrupted Peers,
> > (*First Epistle of the First Book*, 99)
> Faith I shall give the answer Reynard gave,
> "I cannot like, Dread Sir! your Royal Cave;
> "Because I see by all the Tracks about,
> "Full many a Beast goes in, but none comes out,"
> > (*First Epistle of the First Book*, 114-117)
> Rank as the ripeness of a Rabbit's tail,
> > (*Second Satire of the Second Book*, 28)
> Still, still be getting, never, never rest,
> > (*Sixth Epistle of the First Book*, 96)
> And much too wise to walk into a Well.
> > (*Second Epistle of the Second Book*, 191)

86

One source, but by no means a complete explanation, of the conversational quality of the Horatian poems is the frequency of monosyllables and monosyllabic lines; and this is particularly true of
Arbuthnot and the *First Satire of the Second Book*, the most informal of the four poems.[1] *Arbuthnot* especially uses monosyllabic
lines with variety and skill:

If Foes, they write, if Friends, they read me dead, (32)
Of hairs, or straws, or dirt, or grubs, or worms, (170)
Who but must laugh, if such a man there be? (213)
Wit that can creep, and Pride that licks the dust. (333)

Another source of the conversational tone is the normal word
order.[2] In *Arbuthnot*, even such a set piece as the Sporus portrait
has only five inversions in its twenty-five lines (in ll. 311, 312, 315,
317, 330),[3] none violent and two quite evidently for emphasis:

Yet WIT ne'er tastes, and BEAUTY ne'er enjoys, (312)
Eve's Tempter thus the Rabbins have exprest. (330)

And the Atticus portrait, probably the most formal part of the
poem, has only two (ll. 207 and 211), each tucked in almost un-
noticeably amid the straightforward English idiom.

Another contribution to the conversational quality is the infrequency of polysyllables: hardly more than half a dozen in the entire 419 lines of *Arbuthnot*.[4] As well as Pope knew how to use
polysyllables for satire, even the Sporus portrait contains only one
(And he himself one vile Antithesis, l. 325), and three of the
others are in the personal, quite unmocking last part of the poem.

In *Arbuthnot*, Pope's increasing skill at allowing the sense to

1. Monosyllables per line: *Arbuthnot*, 6.37; *First Satire*, 6.33; *Epilogue*,
6.22; *Augustus* (the most formal), 5.98. The relatively informal second *Moral
Essay*, surprisingly, has only 5.56. But contrast the Horatian poems with
Windsor-Forest (5.63), *Messiah* (5.64), *E. on C.* (5.70), *Dunciad* (5.71).
   Monosyllabic lines: *Arbuthnot*, 8 per cent; *First Satire*, 6 per cent; *Epilogue*,
5 per cent; *Augustus*, 4 per cent; *Dunciad*, 2 per cent; *E. on M.*, 4 per cent. Pre-
1717 poems, all below 4 per cent, except *Unfortunate Lady* (6 per cent) and
Eloisa (8 per cent), both monologues.
2. See the long passage from the *First Satire of the Second Book*, quoted on
p. 22, above.
3. Possibly l. 307 should be added, but this slight abnormality could occur
in conversation and sounds conversational.
4. *Arbuthnot*, in 2 per cent of the lines; *First Satire*, 2½ per cent; *Augustus*,
3 per cent. The figure for *Epilogue*, on the other hand, is high (5 per cent),
equalled only by *Eloisa*, *E. on M.*, and the second *Moral Essay*, and exceeded
only by the first *Moral Essay* (7 per cent).

THE REACH OF ART

guide the meter also adds to the colloquial effect. The following line, for example, taken by itself seems to be perfectly regular iambic pentameter except for the light third foot:

Ăll flý tŏ Twít'năm, ànd ĭn húmblĕ stráin. (21)

But when the line is placed in context, the sense requires an initial trochee:

Is there a Parson, much be-mus'd in Beer,
A maudlin Poetess, a ryming Peer,
A Clerk, foredoom'd his Father's soul to cross,
Who pens a Stanza when he should engross?
Is there, who lock'd from Ink and Paper, scrawls
With desp'rate Charcoal round his darken'd walls?

Áll flý tŏ Twít'năm, ànd ĭn húmblĕ stráin
Ăpplý tŏ mĕ, tŏ kéep thĕm mád ŏr váin. (15-22)

An especially colloquial phrase may affect the meter:

Arthur, whose giddy Son neglects the Laws,

Ĭmpútes tŏ-mĕ-ănd-mў-DÁMN'D WÓRKS thĕ cáuse, (23-24)

Ĭ wísh'd thĕ mán ă dínnĕr, ănd SÁTE STÍLL. (152)

Parallelism or antithesis may also vary the emphasis:

Seiz'd and ty'd down to judge, how wretched I!
Who CAN'T be silent, and who WILL not lye, (33-34)
A Lash like mine no HONEST man shall dread,
But all such BABLING BLOCKHEADS in his stead. (303-304)

The opening of *Arbuthnot* is itself the most colloquial of any in Pope, and throughout are lines so informal as to approach the slangy:

The Creature's at his dirty work again, (92)
But wonder how the Devil they got there? (172)
To fetch and carry Sing-song up and down. (226)

As usual in these poems the direct quotations within what is itself dialogue are particularly natural:

"The Piece you think is incorrect: why take it,
"I'm all submission, what you'd have it, make it," (45-46)
"I found him close with Swift"—"Indeed? no doubt"
(Cries prating Balbus) "something will come out." (275-276)

Many lines are run-on, adding to the informal effect; and on the other hand, except in the satirical portraits and in the passages of rising indignation and self-defense toward the end, Pope uses no long series of open couplets. He seems to have considered the deeper flow of such passages ill-suited to conversational tone, and it is of course true that most actual speech falls into comparatively brief segments.

Another contribution to the colloquial tone is the mechanism of dialogue itself. If Arbuthnot speaks, it is nearly always by inter-rupting Pope in mid-sentence; and Pope usually interrupts him back:

Still Sapho—"Hold! for God-sake—you'll offend:
"No Names—be calm—learn Prudence of a Friend:
"I too could write, and I am twice as tall,
"But Foes like these!"—One Flatt'rer's worse than all. (101-104)

Feminine rimes, as usual in Pope, are an indication of infor-mality, and they seem especially conversational when they consist of two words, as in lines 45-46, quoted in a recent paragraph.[5] In-deed, rimes in general, which might seem a hindrance to the effect of speech, are often an actual benefit, in pointing up the normality of the rime word and the word order:

Then from the Mint walks forth the Man of Ryme,
Happy! to catch me, just at Dinner-time, (13-14)
Pitholeon sends to me: "You know his Grace,
"I want a Patron; ask him for a Place."
Pitholeon libell'd me—"but here's a Letter
"Informs you Sir, 'twas when he knew no better. (49-52)

Many such instances occur in passages quoted earlier.

And the questions and exclamations with which the *Epistle to Arbuthnot* is peppered have a quite different effect from those in *An Essay on Man* or *Eloisa to Abelard*. Often casual, brief, play-ful, mock-petulant, they contribute much to the effect of reality. Conversation is not all statement. Especially in such a conversa-tion as this one, in which a man presents a problem to a friend, and the problem is both serious and comic, the rueful query, "What

5. All four of the major Horatian poems have feminine rimes. The finest is probably in *Arbuthnot*:
And he, who now to sense, now nonsense leaning,
Means not, but blunders round about a meaning. (185-186)

89

can I do?" repeated in twenty different ways, is exceedingly natural; and frequent exclamation is certainly not unexpected. The friend, also, ought to ask questions. And parenthesis too, which occurs rather often, is entirely normal in conversation:

Poor guiltless I! and can I chuse but smile,
When ev'ry Coxcomb knows me by my Style? (281-282)
Let Sporus tremble—"What? that Thing of silk,
"Sporus, that mere white Curd of Ass's milk?
"Satire or Sense alas! can Sporus feel?
"Who breaks a Butterfly upon a Wheel?" (305-308)
Has Life no Joys for me? or (to be grave)
Have I no Friend to serve, no Soul to save? (273-274)

And finally, quite apart from special demands of emphasis and meter, the significance of the words often guides tonal pattern and changes in speed, and in an especially colloquial direction. No two people will read a poem with quite the same intonations, but seldom is the way pointed so clearly as at times in Pope's satires; and in such a passage as the following, variations in pitch from reader to reader will probably be a good deal fewer than ordinarily:

Go on, obliging Creatures, make me see
All that disgrac'd my Betters, met in me:
Say for my comfort, languishing in bed,
"Just so immortal Maro held his head:"
And when I die, be sure you let me know
Great Homer dy'd three thousand years ago. (119-124)

Yet along with the colloquial tone, Pope achieves tremendous concentration in *Arbuthnot*. Consider the detail of occurrence and attitude packed (colloquially!) into just one couplet:

If I dislike it, "Furies, death and rage!"
If I approve, "Commend it to the Stage." (57-58)

The latter part of the story of Midas is told with ease and humor in four lines (69-72). A complete tribute to Gay, with its own appropriate tone, is managed gracefully in six (255-260). There is some zeugma, but not a great deal; some foreign usage for condensation, but not a great deal. The abundance of verbs helps (1.39 per line); and one is forced to conclude that the principal method of condensation in *Arbuthnot* is its extremely accurate use of words generally, and of verbs in particular. Fine verbs are a special excellence of the Atticus portrait:

Just hint a fault, and hesitate dislike. (204)

But elsewhere too they are especially apt:

They rave, recite, and madden round the land, (6)
Now trips a Lady, and now struts a Lord. (329)

Of rhetoric, two types attract special attention in *Arbuthnot*. The first is word repetition in various forms, often notably felicitous:

'Tis sung, when Midas' Ears began to spring,
(Midas, a sacred Person and a King), (69-70)
And without sneering, teach the rest to sneer, (202)
The Coxcomb hit, or fearing to be hit. (345)

The other is anticlimax (and occasionally climax):

Poor Cornus sees his frantic Wife elope,
And curses Wit, and Poetry, and Pope, (25-26)
Three things another's modest wishes bound,
My Friendship, and a Prologue, and ten Pound, (47-48)
To help me thro' this long Disease, my Life. (132)

Anticlimax is also achieved by the use of sounds:

Lull'd by soft Zephyrs thro' the broken Pane. (42)

Here the smooth continuants of the first half-line are suddenly "broken" by the explosives of the last half; and the sound as well as the sense informs us that the "soft Zephyrs" are ironical.[6]

In repetition of sound, the poem has all the usual uses of alliteration and assonance, casual and rhetorical, which have become familiar; not by any means as frequently as in, say, *Eloisa to Abelard*, but nevertheless frequently.[7] Certain sounds—*s, p, b, f,* short *i*—occur notably often for satirical effect:

Who shames a *S*cri*b*ler? *b*reak one co*b*we*b* thro',
He *sp*ins the *s*light, *s*elf-*p*leasing thread anew;
De*s*troy hi*s* *F*i*b*, or *So*phi*s*try; *i*n vain, (89-91)
The *B*ard whom *p*il*f*'red *P*astorals renown,
Who turns a *P*ersian Tale for hal*f* a crown,
*J*ust writes to makes his *b*arrenness a*pp*ear,
And strains from hard-*b*ound *b*rains eight lines a-year, (179-182)

---

6. Other excellent examples are in ll. 93-94 and 164.
7. Examples of adjective-substantive alliteration: dire Dilemma (31), sad Civility (37), furious fret (153), pilf'red Pastorals (179), fair Fame (194), foolish face (212), hundred Hawkers (217), babling blockheads (304).

91

> *P*roud, as A*p*ollo on his *f*orked hill,
> Sate *f*ull-*b*lown *B*u*f*o, *p*u*ff*'d by ev'ry quill;
> *F*ed with *s*o*f*t Dedication all day long. (231-233)

This technique is especially noteworthy in the portrait of Sporus; and since this portrait and that of Atticus are probably the most famous in Pope, they deserve special examination. That of Atticus has little repetition of sound or representative meter of any kind. The style is somewhat raised by a steady flow, more open couplets,[8] more resonant sound. A little alliteration is used to point up phrases and parallels:

> Willing to wound, and yet afraid to strike,
> Just hint a fault, and hesitate dislike. (203-204)

In one passage *t*'s and short *i*'s are employed to express littleness and stiff, legalistic precision:

> Like Cato, give his little Senate laws,
> And sit attentive to his own applause. (209-210)

Otherwise the effect of the portrait, so far as versification goes, is in the comparative largeness of tone, which gives the impression that the man himself is not ignoble. Two lines beyond the Atticus portrait occurs the line,

> Or plaister'd posts, with Claps in capitals. (216)

It is surely plain that such a deliberately ugly line would have been completely out of place in the portrait.

On the other hand, probably nothing in all Pope is uglier than the portrait of Sporus. A good many *f*'s and *p*'s occur in connection with unpleasant words, including two of the three definite instances of alliteration:

> In Puns, or Politicks, or Tales, or Lyes, (321)
> Fop at the Toilet, Flatt'rer at the Board. (328)

Another contribution is the obvious and ugly sound repetition of

> This painted Child of Dirt that stinks and stings. (310)

Beginning with line 314 and the word *mumbling*, the sound *m*—

---

8. The whole twenty-two lines of the portrait are a single sentence. (See Root, p. 47.) The portion from the middle of l. 193 to the end of l. 212 consists of two subjunctive clauses, dependent upon the questions in the last two lines (213-214). This fact is obscured by the grammatically impossible period following l. 212 in Tw., which follows the 1st edition.

not a very common sound—is emphasized, appearing at least once in every line save one (and usually in a word of unpleasant significance, such as *impotence, venom, smut*) through line 322. In line 321, the only one in the series without an *m*, the sound *s* begins to be important. The next line is shared between the two sounds:

Or Spite, or Smut, or Rymes, or Blasphemies. (322)

And the rest of the passage hisses almost constantly, with the sound *m*—though it still occurs in unpleasant words, such as *amphibious* and *tempter*—gradually fading out.

Three instances of true representation occur, all of unpleasant sounds or movements: first, the row of indefinite, neutral sounds, illustrative of "mumbling" in

So well-bred Spaniels civilly delight
In mumbling of the Game they dare not bite; (313-314)

next, the abrupt *p*'s, and *t*'s, *k*'s, *s*'s, and long *e*'s, giving a squeaky effect in

Whether in florid Impotence he speaks,
And, as the Prompter breathes, the Puppet squeaks; (317-318)[9]

last, the "see-saw" rhythm in

His Wit all see-saw between that and this,
Now high, now low, now Master up, now Miss. (323-324)

Unlike the Atticus portrait, the passage is divided into several sentences and hence lacks flow. Other qualities contributing to the ugliness include an extremely heavy emphasis on words of unpleasant meaning; rough sound combinations and jerky movement; and in one couplet a deliberate and repellent over-sweetness:

Eternal Smiles his Emptiness betray,
As shallow streams run dimpling all the way. (315-316)

Much of what has been said of the *Epistle to Arbuthnot* applies equally or nearly so to the other three principal satires and epistles. The *Epistle to Arbuthnot* and the *First Satire of the Second Book of Horace* are the closest in material and attitude, and the closest in form. If anything, the *First Satire* is even more colloquial. Of the qualities contributing to the conversational tone of

9. This is an example of word-analysis representation: impotence, squeaks, with the sounds of short *i*, *m*, *p*, *t*, *s*, *k*, and long *e* repeated prominently elsewhere in the couplet.

Arbuthnot, it has all, and in full measure, except the device of sharp interruption and the use of direct quotation within dialogue. It has no stories, no satirical portraits, no open passages of any length. On the other hand, it develops in a few lines a tone which foreshadows—as *Arbuthnot* never does except in the Atticus portrait —the *Epilogue to the Satires:*

> Dash the proud Gamester in his gilded Car,
> Bare the mean Heart that lurks beneath a Star, (107-108)
> To Virtue only and her Friends, a Friend,
> The World beside may murmur, or commend.
> Know, all the distant Din that World can keep
> Rolls o'er my Grotto, and but sooths my Sleep. (121-124)

Like *Arbuthnot,* it begins on a light note; like the *Epilogue,* it ends on one. Otherwise, in versification as in material, it closely resembles the former.

The *Epilogue* also resembles *Arbuthnot.* It has, for instance, the device of interruption (e.g., II, 18-25), intensely colloquial phrases (e.g., I, 38-39; II, 35, 55), and fine monosyllabic lines (e.g., I, 55, 103, 136; II, 8, 19, 123). But Pope's companion in talk in the *Epilogue* is not a friend but an antagonist;[10] and the difference in tone is quite noticeable. Pope is not complaining to a friend, half in jest, half in earnest; he is defending his credit to an adversary, who argues at considerable length—and not unably! He is not sitting quietly in his grotto with a friend interested in his welfare, whose objections are easily overcome. Rather he is faced with the necessity of proving his way of life and work right, with the inescapable corollary of proving the way of his accuser wrong. In consequence, at times the tone is usually grave and comparatively dignified, with a tinge of regret, sometimes raised to anger. In this it somewhat resembles the Atticus portrait; and like that portrait, the *Epilogue* has open passages of considerable length and fine flow; little alliteration or assonance; and especially in the considerable depictions of corruption (for the poem is much less about Pope than about what he sees in the world) a darkness of vowel and consonant matching the material. There is little representative meter[11] or patterning or emphasis for the sake of satire

10. Sherburn, *Best of Pope,* pp. 448-449.
11. One instance:
Silent and soft, as Saints remove to Heav'n,
All Tyes dissolv'd, and ev'ry Sin forgiv'n. (I, 93-94)

on any special sounds. Even the horrid simile of II, 171-180, has, compared to the portrait of Sporus, little ugliness of versification.

But many more polysyllables occur, and they are more often used for satirical effect:

His sly, polite, insinuating stile, (I, 19)
And charitably comfort Knave and Fool. (I, 62)

Finely wrought single lines recall the more formal of the *Essays*:

That "Not to be corrupted is the Shame," (I, 160)
Have still a secret Byass to a Knave. (II, 101)

Exclamation and interrogation are used more often with serious intent than in *Arbuthnot* or the *First Satire*. There is little or no anticlimax.

Still, the similarities remain more remarkable than the differences. In the *Epilogue to the Satires*, Pope applies the colloquial speech, the condensation by accurate and frequent verbs,[12] to much the same material as before, but in a graver mood and situation. The differences in technique are those essential to mark that change.

The *Epistle to Augustus* is the least typical of this group of satires and epistles in that it is not a dialogue, and its subject matter is somewhat off to one side. (The material is not altogether unlike, since the problems and purposes of satire are brought up and various corruptions of the times pointed out.) Yet its tone is usually informal, occasionally quite colloquial (e.g., ll. 61-62, 79-80, 188), and never so serious as the most serious couplets or passages of the other three. On the other hand, the mockery of its exclamations and of its passages of heightened tone (as well as its anticlimaxes) resembles the mockery of *The Rape of the Lock*:

Oh! could I mount on the Maeonian wing,
Your Arms, your Actions, your Repose to sing!
What seas you travers'd! and what fields you fought!
Your Country's Peace, how oft, how dearly bought!
How barb'rous rage subsided at your word,
And Nations wonder'd while they dropp'd the sword!
How, when you nodded, o'er the land and deep,
Peace stole her wing, and wrapt the world in sleep;
Till earth's extremes your mediation own,
And Asia's Tyrants tremble at your Throne. (394-403)

12. E.g.: Some rising Genius *sins up* to my Song (II, 9). *Epilogue* has the highest verb rate of any of the major poems.

The poem has open passages of considerable length; it has, like the others of its group, much enjambment; it makes comparatively little use of interrogation or exclamation, but uses parenthesis effectively to add to the conversational tone; direct quotation once again contributes to condensation and informality; it has the usual fine verbs; it makes rather more use than the others of casual alliteration; like *Arbuthnot*, it makes fine use of word repetition (e.g., ll. 79, 87, 235-236, 287, 406-407), anticlimax (e.g., ll. 45-48, 295, 395, 397), and the piling on of certain sounds for satirical effect (e.g., the *p*'s in ll. 293-295); and its ending (ll. 416-419) comes particularly close to the matter and the tone of the *Epistle to Arbuthnot* and the *First Satire*. Again the differences in technique are largely such as to make the tone fit the material and mood, though here the tone is perhaps unexpectedly colloquial. But of all the major poems before 1717, *An Essay on Criticism* was most colloquial in tone. The *Epistle to Augustus*, dealing with somewhat similar materials, resembles *An Essay on Criticism* in its degree of informality.

II

As the *Epistle to Augustus* recalls *An Essay on Criticism*, so *The Dunciad*[13] recalls *The Rape of the Lock*. Both, of course, are mock-heroic. Both make much use of anticlimax.[14] Both employ various epic conventions, such as the announcement of the subject,[15] the use of the conventional Homeric statements following quoted speech (e.g., I, 319), and epic similes (e.g., II, 247 ff.). And both poems imitate *Paradise Lost*, deliberately and plainly, *The Rape of the Lock* most clearly in Ariel's address to the sylphs,

13. This discussion is based on *Dunciad* B.
14. Sometimes in a very similar way:
Let Spades be Trumps! she said, and Trumps they were,
                                                    (*Rape of the Lock*, III, 46)
Europe he saw, and Europe saw him too. (*Dunciad*, IV, 294)
Cf. also *Rape of the Lock*, I, 16, and *Dunciad*, I, 93-94. As in *The Rape of the Lock*, there are anticlimactical lists—e.g., I, 88. More often, however, *The Dunciad*'s anticlimax is of its own peculiar kind:
All Flesh is humbled, Westminster's bold race
Shrink, and confess the Genius of the place:
The pale Boy-Senator yet tingling stands,
And holds his breeches close with both his hands. (IV, 145-148)
Other examples: I, 90; II, 286; III, 312; IV, 34.
15. The formula is exactly the same: subject in the first two lines, "I sing" beginning the third. But it is more abrupt and anticlimactical in *The Dunciad*.

The Dunciad in the opening of Book II, in which Cibber takes Satan's place, "High on a gorgeous seat." But the difference between these two Miltonic echoes is a mark of the difference in the poems; and in tone and meter *The Dunciad* resembles *The Rape of the Lock* less than the second *Moral Essay* does. In the *Rape of the Lock*, Ariel follows Satan in his method of calling together the supernatural powers, but the comparison is not invidious. Ariel's call is smaller, it is infinitely less significant; but the imitation is of Milton's style, little more. In *The Dunciad*, the comparison is grotesque;[16] the new occupant of a high throne is a producer of evil (as Ariel was not), but in how small and ridiculous a way! As Satan's summoning of the fallen angels was tremendous, Ariel's call to the sylphs was charming; as Satan's throne was resplendently evil, Cibber's is ugly, absurd, and attended by small, repellent, negative sins.

The Dunciad is in fact unique among Pope's poems; and it is another demonstration of Pope's fitting style to matter that its technique resembles in one way or another the technique of almost every major poem in the canon, in some ways resembles that of none of them, and is finally and distinctly itself. Alliteration, assonance, and representative meter are used in an abundance and variety seen nowhere else later than *Eloisa to Abelard*. *The Rape of the Lock*'s purposeful obviousness reappears; a whole flood of the ugliness of the Sporus portrait in the *Epistle to Arbuthnot*, and the intentional oversweetness of many passages in the late poems. Certain specific sounds are repeated for satire, as in *Arbuthnot*. The greatly heightened conclusion recalls the *Messiah*. In extreme contrast to *The Rape of the Lock*, the vowels and consonants are even darker than in *An Essay on Man*. In spite of the comparative formality, an occasional colloquialism pops out, as in the satires and epistles (e.g., I, 165, 189, 300; II, 178); yet monosyllabic lines occur less frequently than in any other poem later than the *Messiah*, and are relatively unremarkable. As elsewhere, Pope uses the polysyllable for satirical purposes, though not so often, nor so superbly, as might have been expected:

Furious he dives, precipitately dull, (II, 316)
A Fiend in glee, ridiculously grim. (III, 154)

16. Another very noticeable imitation is
On feet and wings, and flies, and wades, and hops, (II, 64)
again of Satan, again grotesque.

The verb count is the lowest of that in any major poem, but as in the other late poems, some verbs are of unusual excellence:

New edge their dulness, and *new bronze* their face, (II, 10)
Prompt or to *guard* or *stab*, to *saint* or *damn*. (II, 357)

But, in spite of a quite frequent zeugma, the scarce verbs are indicative of a lesser degree of condensation than in the other late poems.

In rhetoric, *The Dunciad* has no special outstanding type except anticlimax. Chiasmus appears, as always, but (as in the other late poems) not very noticeably; there is fine anaphora, but relatively little of it; much parenthesis, as in all the satirical poems, but without much effect. *The Dunciad* does demonstrate, as all the late poems demonstrate, Pope's skill at word repetition:

What then remains? Ourself. Still, still remain
Cibberian forehead, and Cibberian brain, (I, 217-218)
Joy fills his soul, joy innocent of thought, (III, 249)
A wit with dunces, and a dunce with wits, (IV, 90)
So may the sons of sons of sons of whores. (IV, 332)

Yet even word repetition does not occur so frequently—nor so felicitously—as in some of the late poems.

Pope does achieve frequently in *The Dunciad* the long open passages, and the flow, of *An Essay on Man*, as well as remarkably fine caesural variety and enjambment.[17] But like *Eloisa to Abelard* and *An Essay on Man*, the poem displays, over and above the variations in tone and speed from passage to passage, a sameness of tone that is unfortunate. We are asked too often to "see" somebody or other make a fool of himself, to "see" good things thrust aside by dull; the present tense itself grows tiresome; and, as in *Eloisa*, the *Messiah*, and *An Essay on Man*, there is an overabundance of exclamation.

The most distinctive and prominent of *The Dunciad*'s qualities—the ones which serve most to set it apart from Pope's other major poems—are its repetition of sound and its representative meter. Alliterative epithets are everywhere. In Book I alone, an incom-

---

17. An occasional overflowing of the couplet resembles that in the early pastoral poems, e.g.:
To move, to raise, to ravish ev'ry heart,
With Shakespear's nature, or with Johnson's art,
Let others aim. (*Dunciad*, II, 223-225)
Other examples: I, 155-157; I, 289-291; II, 103-105.

plete list includes Mighty Mother (1), fam'd father (31), brazen, brainless brothers (32), new-born nonsense (60), ductile dulness (64), hoary hills (75), heavy harvests (78), momentary monsters (83), broad banners (88), City Swans (96), poor page (105), mighty Mad (106), native night (176), curious cobweb (180), brazen Brightness (219), smutty sisters (230), Birth-day brand (245), high-born Howard (297). Other notable examples are, from Book II, motley mixture (21), meagre, muse-rid mope (37), shapeless shade (111), dark dexterity (278), plunging Prelate (323); from Book III, slip-shod Sibyl (15) (probably the best of the lot), funereal Frown (152), sable Sorc'rer (233); from Book IV, pompous page (114), Greek grammarians (215), Syren Sisters (541), sturdy Squire (595). And alliterative epithets are only a small portion of the alliteration in the poem. The alliterative letter may appear again—and again—and again:

Laborious, heavy, *b*usy, *b*old, and *b*lind, (I, 15)
She sees a *M*ob of *M*etaphors advance,
Pleas'd with the *m*adness of the *m*azy dance, (I, 67-68)
While *p*ensive *P*oets *p*ainful vigils keep, (I, 93)
With Fool of *Q*uality compleats the *q*uire, (I, 298)
By *h*erald *H*awkers, *h*igh *h*eroic Games, (II, 18)
All as a *p*artridge *p*lump, *f*ull-*f*ed, and *f*air, (II, 41)
And Demonstration *th*in, and *Th*eses *th*ick, (II, 241)
Long Chanc'ry-lane *r*etentive *r*olls the sound,
And courts to courts *r*eturn it *r*ound and *r*ound;
Thames wafts it thence to *R*ufus' *r*oaring hall, (II, 263-265)
Slow rose a form, in *m*ajesty of *M*ud, (II, 326)
A low-*b*orn, *c*ell-*b*red, *s*elfish, *s*ervile *b*and, (II, 356)[18]
*M*eek *m*odern faith to *m*urder, hack, and *m*awl, (III, 210)
For *w*riting *P*amphlets, and for *r*oasting *P*opes, (III, 284)
*M*ad *M*athesis alone was unconfin'd,
Too *m*ad for *m*ere *m*aterial chains to bind, (IV, 31-32)
His *b*eaver'd *b*row a *b*irchen garland wears, (IV, 141)
*S*o *s*pins the *s*ilk-worm *s*mall its *s*lender *s*tore, (IV, 253)
And titt'ring *p*ush'd the *P*edants off the *p*lace, (IV, 276)
False as his *G*ems, and *c*anker'd as his *C*oins,
*C*ame, *c*ramm'd with *c*apon, (IV, 349-350)
"*G*rant, *g*racious *G*oddess! *g*rant me still to cheat." (IV, 355)

These are only a few of the more obvious, extreme examples.

18. In "*cell*-bred, *sel*fish" this line has also an example of the obvious syllabic repetition commented on below, p. 101.

The repetition of consonant sounds, not only initially, but internally, is never-ending; and (as in *Arbuthnot*, but to a far greater extent) certain specific sounds appear with remarkable frequency throughout all four books of *The Dunciad*. This is apparent even in the examples of extreme alliteration just quoted. The quotations were chosen for their aptness, not to illustrate the alliteration of any particular sound, yet of the twenty-one instances of alliterated sounds in the quotations, five sounds—*b, f, m, p, s*—account for fourteen alliterations.[19] And it is these five sounds which appear with most notable frequency throughout—very often, as in the portrait of Sporus in *Arbuthnot*, to put special emphasis on words of unpleasant meaning. Of the 330 lines in Book I, at least 150 are involved in noticeable repetition of one or more of the five sounds; other examples from Books I and II, as intricate and various as they are frequent, include:

She *s*aw *s*low Philip*s* cree*p* like Tate'*s poor p*age,
And all the *m*ighty *M*ad in Denni*s* rage.
In each she *m*ark*s* her I*m*age *f*ull expre*s*t,
But chie*f* in Bay*s*'s *m*on*s*ter-*b*reeding *b*reast, (I, 105-108) [20]
Here lay *p*oor *F*letcher's hal*f*-eat *s*cenes, and here
The Fri*pp*ery of cru*c*i*f*y'd Moliere;
There ha*pless* Shake*s*pear, yet of Ti*bb*ald *s*ore,
Wish'd he had *b*lotted for him*s*el*f b*e*f*ore, (I, 131-134)
There, *s*av'd by *s*pice, like *M*u*mm*ies, *m*any a year, (I, 151)
E'er *s*ince *S*ir Fo*p*ling's *P*eriwig was *P*raise,
To the la*s*t honours of the *B*utt and *B*ays:

---

19. This is also true of twenty of the thirty adjective-substantive alliterations quoted just before. Tillotson (pp. 141-142) notes the frequency of alliteration but emphasizes somewhat different sounds.

20. Note that even the more uncommon of the five sounds is likely to occur at least once (and prominently) in each passage, even if it happens not to be one of the frequently repeated sounds in that passage. Examples: the prominent *ph* (*f*) of *Philips* in the first couplet of this passage; the prominent *m* of *Moliere* in the next passage; the prominent *f* of *Fopling* in the fourth; the repeated if not prominent *m*'s of *whelms, flames,* and *ample* in the fifth; the *b* of *Cibber* in the sixth. The sound *s* would be less noticeable, perhaps, without frequent repetition; but even *s* (that is, the unvoiced *s*, as opposed to the "voiced *s*" or *z*) occurs less frequently than might be supposed in ordinary writing, since the letter *s* is very frequently voiced in its common uses: *is, was, these, those, his,* and all regular plurals of nouns and third person singular present tenses of verbs except of words ending in *f, k, p,* or *t*. Hence it does not take many *s*'s to make a passage "hiss," and Pope often throws into such passages the extra fillip of the closely related *sh* sound.

O thou! of *Bus'ness* the directing *soul!*
To thi*s* our head like *b*ya*ss* to the *b*owl, (I, 167-170)
*S*udden she *f*lies, and whelms it o'er the *p*yre;
Down *s*ink the *f*lames, and with a hi*ss* ex*p*ire.
Her am*p*le *p*re*s*ence *f*ills u*p* all the *p*lace;
A veil of *f*ogs dilate*s* her aw*f*ul *f*ace, (I, 259-262)
Great *C*ibber *s*ate: The *p*roud *P*arna*ss*ian *s*neer,
The con*s*ciou*s* *s*im*p*er, and the jealou*s* leer,
*M*i*x* on his look, (II, 5-7)
Our *p*urging*s*, *p*um*p*ings, *b*lankettings, and *b*lows, (II, 154)
While thu*s* each hand *p*romote*s* the *p*leasing *p*ain,
And quick *s*en*s*ations *s*ki*p* from vein to vein,
A youth unknown to *P*hoebu*s*, in de*s*pair,
*P*uts his la*s*t re*f*uge all in heav'n and *p*ray'r.
What *f*orce have *p*iou*s* vows! (II, 211-215)
Denni*s* and Di*ss*onan*c*e, and ca*p*tiou*s* Art,
And *S*ni*p-s*na*p* short, and Interru*p*tion *s*mart, (II, 239-240)
In naked *m*ajesty Old*m*i*x*on *s*tands,
And *M*ilo-like *s*urveys his ar*m*s and hands. (II, 283-284)

Other fine examples are in III, 139-142, 251-255, 317-318; and IV, 79-80, 120-121, 595-596. Again this is only a selection of the more extreme instances. And I have tried, in so far as possible, to avoid cases which intermingle the patterning of other consonant sounds with the principal five. Add these—and there are many of them; add the separate patterning of sounds other than the principal five; add the almost endless more casual repetitions: and one sees how consonant repetition in general, and of five sounds particularly, accounts in large measure for the special texture of *The Dunciad.*

But Pope also employs in *The Dunciad* another and unusual sort of deliberately obvious sound repetition: repetition of syllables, usually but not always initial:

*Em*blem of Music caus'd by *Em*ptiness, (I, 36)
O! pass more *in*nocent, *in* *in*fant state, (I, 237)
With reams *a*bundant this *a*bode supply, (II, 90)
*A*ppear'd *A*pollo's May'r and Aldermen, (IV, 116)
And well dis*sem*bled *em*'rald on his hand,
False as his *Gem*s. (IV, 348-349)[21]

---

21. Note also the two somewhat similar and extreme sorts of obviousness:
Th'unconscious stream sleeps o'er thee *like* a *lake*, (II, 304)
Men bearded, bald, cowl'd, uncowl'd, shod, unshod,
Peel'd, patch'd, and pyebald. (III, 114-115)

With so very much emphasis upon consonantal repetition, vowel repetition (assonance), frequent as it is in *The Dunciad*, passes largely unnoticed. One exception is the short *u*. Short *u* occurs in both *dullness* and *dunce*; it has a neutral sound which is itself dull and flat; and by chance or by some linguistic instinct, it occurs in the language in numerous words of unpleasant connotation, especially monosyllables. For all these reasons, it occurs frequently and very noticeably in *The Dunciad*:

> And suck'd all o'er, like an industrious Bug, (I, 130)
> Not sail, with Ward, to Ape-and-monkey climes,
> Where vile Mundungus trucks for viler rhymes, (I, 233-234) [22]
> Then number'd with the puppies in the mud, (II, 308)
> The clam'rous crowd is hush'd with mugs of Mum, (II, 385)
> As what a Dutchman plumps into the lakes. (II, 405)[23]

Thus the ugliness of sound which characterized the portrait of *Sporus* in *Arbuthnot* is almost constant in *The Dunciad*. Probably the most unpleasant example (and it is not merely the nauseating imagery: the similar passage in *Epilogue to the Satires*, II, 171-180, is not nearly so ugly-sounding) is the passage on Curll's fall, II, 102-106.[24]

On the other hand, at least one instance occurs of elaborate *pleasant* sound patterning—so elaborate as to assist greatly in "representing" the description of languid decadence:

> To Isles of fragrance, lilly-silver'd vales,

l f r ā g r s l ĭ l s ĭ l v r v ā l

> Diffusing languor in the panting gales:

d ĭ f ĭ ng ă ng g r ă n ĭ ng g l

> To lands of singing, or of dancing slaves,

l ă n s ĭ ng ĭ ng d ă n s ĭ ng s l v

22. As here, and in several other of the passages quoted, the sound occurs very frequently in combinations with *m*'s. Note also the similar technique in the initial vowels of
With cow-like udders, and with ox-like eyes, (II, 164)
and the appearance of words with such sounds in extremely emphatic locations as in
Loud thunder to its *bottom* shook the bog. (I, 329)
23. A good idea of the wide variation in Pope's prosody may be obtained by comparing this image of circles in water (II, 405-410), with the same image in *E. on M.*, IV, 363-372.
24. Note also the comically ugly effect of using precisely the wrong sounds:
So from the Sun's broad beam, in shallow urns. (II, 11)

Love-whisp'ring woods, and lute-resounding waves.

l v w ĭ s ĭ ng w l d ĭ ng w v   (IV, 303-306)

In fact, Pope uses more representative meter in *The Dunciad* than in any other late poem. And he uses representative meter more often than anywhere else for humorous purposes.[25] Many of the passages already quoted provide examples; further examples, humorous and otherwise, include:

Obliquely wadling to the mark in view, (I, 172)
And cackling save the Monarchy of Tories, (I, 212)
Drowns the loud clarion of the braying Ass, (II, 234)
Then down-are-roll'd-the-books; stretch'd o'er 'em lies
Each gentle clerk, and mutt'ring seals his eyes, (II, 403-404)
Some strain in rhyme; the Muses, on their racks,
Scream like the winding of ten thousand jacks. (III, 159-160)

Two long passages of constant use of representative meter are the falling asleep at the end of Book II and the description of the "mincing Harlot" extolling opera, near the beginning of Book IV.

But repetition of sound and representative meter could not alone sustain a poem the length of *The Dunciad*. They are not the only techniques, they are simply the most prominent. Other techniques have been mentioned: the dark tone quality, the frequent strong flow. And Pope in *The Dunciad* again displays many of those perfectly wrought lines that, in his later years especially, he fashioned with consummate skill (e.g., I, 52, 189, 300; II, 278; III, 16; IV, 76).

In summary, then, the outstanding technical qualities of *The Dunciad* are: (1) first and overwhelmingly, its use of repetition of sound, especially of *b*, *f*, *m*, *p*, *s* and short *u*; (2) its representative meter; (3) its purposely ugly, and often comic, sound combinations and metrical emphasis upon words of unpleasant meaning; (4) its purposeful, and often comic, overfacility of sound and meter, resembling the method of *The Rape of the Lock*; (5) its caesural variety; (6) its frequent use, especially in contrast to *The Rape of the Lock*, of middle and back vowels and voiced consonants, and its consequent heavier texture and darker tone; (7) its long open passages and flow.

The Dunciad lacks the superb proportion of Pope's other mock-

25. See p. 32, above.

heroic poem, and it lacks sufficient variety to escape monotony. The parts are in some respects superior to the whole. Yet as in that other mock-heroic, Pope achieves in *The Dunciad* a singleness of effect—an effect this time not of charm or of elegant mockery, but of something different. The very weight of the poem's dark sounds, the persistence of its alliteration, the grotesqueness of its comedy, the mass of its detail, the frequency of saying the same thing in different ways (and often in themselves superb ways), the basic flow: all contribute to an effect providing an otherwise inadequate bass in Pope's orchestration, an effect which, based as it so largely is on accumulation and repetition, somewhat resembles that of two other major eighteenth-century works, *The Journal of the Plague Year* and *Clarissa*. That effect is of power. Without *The Dunciad*—in spite of the close of the *Messiah*, and many passages in *An Essay on Man* and the epistles and satires—one would feel less confident in attributing such a quality to Pope's work. But *The Dunciad*, whatever its flaws, has power. It is a strange power, grotesque and in some respects repellent. But it is surely there.

*   *   *   *   *

And so Pope did what all great poets do: take a form, stamp their individuality upon it, make it do what they desire. With representative meter, he could perform wonders; and, in spite of Johnson's doubts, those who come to Pope believing representation to be a sharply circumscribed technique, will leave, if unprejudiced, with their eyes opened. If his achievement of tight condensation without loss of smoothness or clarity is a great accomplishment, his achievement of a colloquial tone within so narrow a verse form and so condensed a thought sequence is perhaps a greater. The variety of his verses is astonishingly wide: subtle variations in tone color, in caesural quality and quantity, in the weight of a line and the beats within it; unusual lightness and swiftness, unusual heaviness and sonority; fine, gradual, effortless crescendos and diminuendos. One of his major skills, not always recognized, is in making the sense guide the meter. Another, and a dazzling one, is in turning all sorts of techniques and elements of verse—caesura, enjambment, rime, polysyllables, meter, representation, sound patterning, interrogation, exclamation, parenthesis—to the purposes of satire. And he did far more interlacing of couplets into complex verse paragraphs, employed far more non-central caesuras, and made more use (and successful use) of non-iambic feet than he has usually received credit for. For he had the skill all great poets have, the skill he extolled in *An Essay on Criticism*, to obey rules with artistry and to break them with grace.

So in the end, what he did was what he always said a poet should do: make the sound match the sense, make the style vary constantly and accurately with the material. We may quarrel at times, in our very different century, with his choice of material or with its somewhat limited range. Occasionally we may quarrel, as in *Eloisa to Abelard* or *The Dunciad*, with some aspects of the style he believed suitable to it. But he does carry out his theory almost unfailingly, not only from poem to poem but within the poems. And at his best the result is various, apt, convincing, flexible, organic, and remarkably entertaining.

Little more can be asked of a system of versification than that.

UNIVERSITY OF FLORIDA MONOGRAPHS

HUMANITIES

No. 1. (Spring 1959): *The Uncollected Letters of James Gates Percival.* Edited by Harry R. Warfel

No. 2 (Fall 1959): *Leigh Hunt's Autobiography The Earliest Sketches.* Edited by Stephen F. Fogle

No. 3 (Winter 1960): *Pause Patterns in Elizabethan and Jacobean Drama.* By Ants Oras

No. 4 (Spring 1960): *Rhetoric and American Poetry of the Early National Period.* By Gordon E. Bigelow

No. 5 (Fall 1960): *The Background of The Princess Casamassima.* By W. H. Tilley

No. 6 (Winter 1961): *Indian Sculpture in the John and Mable Ringling Museum of Art* By Roy C. Craven, Jr.

No. 7 (Spring 1961): *The Cestus. A Mask* Edited by Thomas B. Stroup

No. 8 (Fall 1961): Tamburlaine, Part I *and Its Audience.* By Frank B. Fieler

No. 9 (Winter 1962): *The Case of John Darrell Minister and Exorcist.* By Corinne Holt Rickert

No. 10 (Spring 1962): *Reflections of the Civil War in Southern Humor.* By Wade H. Hall

No. 11 (Fall 1962): *Charles Dodgson Semeiotician.* By Daniel F. Kirk

No. 12 (Winter 1963): *Three Middle English Religious Poems.* Edited by R. H. Bowers

No. 13 (Spring 1963): *The Existentialism of Miguel de Unamuno.* By José Huertas-Jourda

No. 14 (Fall 1963): *Four Spiritual Crises in Mid-Century American Fiction.* By Robert Detweiler

No. 15 (Winter 1964): *Style and Society in German Literary Expressionism.* By Egbert Krispyn

No. 16 (Spring 1964): *The Reach of Art: A Study in the Prosody of Pope.* By Jacob H. Adler